MARGINALIZATION of the BLACK MALE

MARGINALIZATION of the BLACK MALE

Insights from the Development of the Teaching Profession

Second Edition

ERROL MILLER

Canoe PRESS

Barbados Jamaica Trinidad and Tobago

Canoe Press University of the West Indies
1A Aqueduct Flats Mona
Kingston 7 Jamaica

Published 1994. Second edition
Printed in Jamaica
ISBN 976 8125 04 7

98 97 96 95 94 6 5 4 3 2

CATALOGUING IN PUBLICATION DATA

Miller, Errol
Marginalization of the black male: insights from the development of the teaching profession / Errol Miller. - 2d ed. rev.

p. cm.
Includes bibliographical references.
ISBN 976 8125 04 7
1. Educational sociology – Jamaica – History. 2. Marginality, social – in Jamaica – History. 3. Sex discrimination in education – Jamaica – History.
4. Teachers – Jamaica – History. I. Title.
LC191.8.J3M54 1994 370.19'097292-dc-20

Set in 10 / 12 Palatino x 27

Cover design by Prodesign Ltd
Page design by Karen Holloway
Printed and bound by Stephenson's LithoPress Ltd

CONTENTS

List of Illustrations

Figures

List of Tables

Preface

Marginalization of the Black Male, as the title implies, focuses on black males but the point is repeatedly made that male marginalization is not peculiar to Blacks, but that it is a phenomenon most noticeable among Blacks because they have been a subordinate group that has mounted a sustained challenge concerning its position in society.

Underpinning this study is a new theory of society, the theory of place. This theory asserts that society is organized on the basis of place: the relative positions of individuals and groups with respect to power, resources, status, belief and culture. Place is a unitary entity comprised of these five dimensions. Hence, no aspect of society can be understood solely in terms of any one of the dimensions, although one dimension may contribute more than the others in a particular society in a specific period.

According to this theory, an egalitarian society is a utopian ideal that can never be achieved in reality. Relative inequality is the reality of society. Places in society are therefore scattered between centre and margin. At any particular moment in time, some individuals and groups in society will be more central and others more marginal.

The real dilemma in human society, however, is that the relative inequality which is the reality cannot be absolutely or permanently justified. The continuing and persistent dialectic in society is that the egalitarian ideal which is inherently just is a practical impossibility, while the relative inequality which is the practical reality is inherently arbitrary and unjust. This is the dynamic in society that fosters change.

Society and community cannot operate without structure, that is, some basis on which to justify or allocate inequality. Societies therefore invent criteria to allocate and justify inequality. These criteria are put forward as if they were the only right and rational basis for determining the relative relations of individuals and groups in society, while at the same time they are no more than the temporary bases on which inequality is justified at a particular time.

Accordingly, over the long haul of history, place in society is being forever contested and the basis of societal organization is perennially challenged. Consequently, the basis of rationalizing inequality is repeatedly renegotiated. Hence marginality and centrality are not permanent or terminal locations, but interchangeable positions in society.

In *Marginalization of the Black Male,* the theory of place is used to identify race, class, gender and age as the operational absolutes employed in allocating inequality in Jamaica. Hypotheses are then generated dealing with gender changes among elementary school teachers and teachers' college students over the period 1837 to 1990. Elementary school teaching and teachers' college students were selected because they represent the major means of upward social mobility open to Blacks since the abolition of slavery.

This work demonstrates both empirically and theoretically how manipulation of the structure of opportunities contributes to changing the socialization patterns of the home and the school from patterns favouring the achievement of boys to that of girls. It offers new insights and a fresh approach to puzzling developments that are increasingly engaging the attention of the public, parents and policy makers alike.

In essence, the difference between the original and this second edition is that here I have stated the theory which I have been employing in exploring gender in society. Chapters one, two and five are more or less new and specifically address the theoretical issues. As such, these chapters seek to establish the general significance of the study and its applicability outside of the Jamaican or Caribbean context.

The original edition is by and large preserved as chapter three, with relatively modest additions of new information, and is treated as it really is: a Jamaican case study. Chapter four substantially expands the data and findings with respect to the long-term impact of changes in the structure of opportunity on gender shifts in education in Jamaica.

My hope is that those who found the first edition interesting and insightful will find this edition a more complete explanation of the phenomenon of male marginalization in society. The hope is, also, that readers will come to appreciate that male marginalization is not peculiar or unique to black or Jamaican men. Most importantly, I trust that this study will help to advance the study of gender, rather than women's or men's issues, and that its relations to race, age and class will be better understood.

ERROL MILLER
1993

Preface to the First Edition

This publication is significant in two respects. First, it focuses on a topic germane to an understanding of the process of education and educational policy in a colonial society. These, in turn, have implications for issues related to gender relations which are currently receiving much attention among anthropologists and sociologists as well as researchers in the area of women's studies. Professor Miller's thesis on the marginalization of the black male in many ways challenges orthodoxy and raises several pertinent issues concerning the future of education in Jamaica. He marshalls the historical material and empirical data in an exciting manner that is bound to provoke lively debate among academics and practitioners.

The auspices of the work are equally important. It is a revised version of the **Inaugural Aubrey Phillips Memorial Lecture**, delivered by Professor Miller, under the sponsorship of the Faculty of Education, University of the West Indies, Mona, on 30 April 1986. The uniqueness and incisiveness of Professor Miller's analysis is, indeed, a fitting way to commemorate the path-breaking contribution to education by the late Professor Aubrey Phillips.

The Institute [of Social and Economic Research] is very pleased to have collaborated in the production of this publication which, in part, emerges out of an ISER project on the Sociology of Education in Jamaica being undertaken by Professor Miller in his capacity as an Associate Research Fellow. It also provides us with an opportunity to identify with a tangible tribute to the late Professor Phillips as an admirable and outstanding scholar, educator and gentleman. We wish to thank the International Development Research Council of Canada (IDRC) for supporting the sociology of education project and UNESCO Paris for contributing to the cost of this publication.

J Edward Greene
Director, ISER
1986

ACKNOWLEDGEMENTS

I wish to thank Ms Linda Cameron and The Press University of the West Indies for this opportunity to revise and update *Marginalization of the Black Male* in a second edition. The original edition has a special place in my sentiments, for it marks my first attempt to publicly report my research on gender with special reference to men. At the same time, this first effort suffered in some ways from my shaky confidence in departing from conventional positions as well as my own timidity in not boldly stating the theoretical basis for that departure. This second edition attempts to address these limitations.

I wish to thank the Institute of Social and Economic Research and its Director, Dr Elsie Le Franc, for giving permission to me to have this second edition published by The Press UWI. I am grateful to Miss Carlene Thomas for entering the first edition on diskette thus easing my task in both revising the text and making the planned additions. Many thanks to my friend and colleague, Professor Elsa Leo-Rhynie, for reading chapters one and two, and particularly for her constructive comments and observations.

MARGINALIZATION of the BLACK MALE

1

Problems and Explanations

DEFINING THE PROBLEM

"Why are black men not working?" asks Louis (1985) in *Essence* magazine. Black men in America seem almost an endangered species states Munroe (1987) in *Newsweek* magazine. "Where have all the men gone?" asks Carl Wint (1989) in Jamaica. "Being a real man – like Mom", writes Sharbodie (1992) in the *Trinidad Guardian*. "The Crisis of the Black Male" is the theme of the *Black Scholar* journal of May/June 1987.

These feature articles and columns by journalists and scholars constitute evidence of the growing perception and disquiet about the social situation of black men in American and Caribbean societies. While some state their concern in more sober and measured tones, others do so in more apocalyptic and sombre terms, sounding an alarm.

The sources of concern often cited relate to the family and home, the school, employment and the workplace, the church and cults, and gangs, crime and violence. Each of these require some expansion and explanation.

Black men, as fathers, are increasingly absent from the home. The black family is often stereotyped as fatherless. The claim is that even where some are present in the home they are ineffective in the father role. This could be described as "hidden fatherlessness" as the physical presence of the man is not matched by the performance of the social role. The result is that an increasing number of black households are headed by their women and not their men, even when the men are physically present. In addition, the single mother struggling to raise her children is a well known phenomenon among Blacks. So-called black male irresponsibility is often cited as the cause of these forms of family organization.

Black boys are said to be fast becoming the second sex in schools. They often start school later, attend more irregularly, drop out earlier and attain much lower levels of educational achievement than black girls. This pattern is now evident at all levels of the education system: primary or elementary, secondary and tertiary. While among most other ethnic groups, on the whole, more women are illiterate than men, among blacks the reverse is true: more men are illiterate than women. Generally, black women are better educated than black men.

One explanation often given for the poor school performance of black boys is that they are not interested in school and education because they think that they can get by without them. They exploit opportunities outside of the "system" for which formal education is not a requirement. They do not therefore apply themselves as diligently as black girls whose future largely depends on making good in school. On the other hand, black girls are said to be more conforming to the "system" and its designated channels of upward social mobility through education. This explanation does not deal with why there are such gender differences among blacks in the "system", whatever that is.

Among young black men it is often more meaningful to speak of unemployment than employment since they constitute the bulk of the jobless. Some say that this is so because most of them are unemployable. They possess limited basic education, they are unskilled, they have little or no understanding of the work ethic and their general attitudes and habits are not consistent with those required to be productive at the work place.

Black men are increasingly absent from the church, and especially alienated from mainstream and orthodox religions. They express their religious convictions mainly in cults that are variants of universalist religions, whether Christian or Muslim. Orthodox religions are increasingly peopled by black women. The absence of the men from the mainstream churches is often interpreted as signs of their deviance and sinfulness.

One portrayal of black men is that they predominate in gangs, violence and crimes of all sorts. They are overrepresented among those arrested and imprisoned. They are overrepresented among drug pushers and among those on death row. The greatest cause of death among black men between the ages of fifteen and fifty is justifiable or unjustifiable homicide. Violent death, by their peers or the police, is the greatest single threat to their daily existence. To black men the streets are mean, but it is the centre of their existence.

This portrayal purports that black men predominate in illegitimate activities in society. Many of those not involved in crime are often involved in self destructive activities like the abuse of alcohol or hard drugs. The older ones seem to espouse a rum bar or liquor store culture, while the younger ones prefer gangs, cocaine or crack. Those who seek to escape this fate enrol in the military or police where they also become exposed to high risks. However, in these instances their invidious position is masked by notions of legitimacy and noble ends, defending society from without and within.

Black men constitute part of the hard core of the growing underclass that has emerged in depressed urban communities—whether these are called ghettos or inner city areas. As such they are feared and suspected persons, which can be a crime in some societies. They are chief among the original homeless people in society. They are overrepresented among the insane on the streets. In most cities in the United States young black men have a greater chance of ending up in jail or pushing drugs than of getting a job or going to college.

In addition, while several intervention programmes are focused on mediating the conditions of women and children in depressed urban communities, few programmes are developed to address the specific issues confronting black men. The condition among black men is often perceived as hopeless and beyond remedy.

Many persons reject this negative portrayal of the black man and point to his exploitation in the New World. They maintain that the positive achievements of black men are being downplayed while the negative is being overplayed. They point to the significant progress made by blacks in the postwar period and recite the honour roll of eminent black men to be found in all spheres of public endeavour. This is particularly so in the Caribbean where many black men have assumed the highest political office as presidents and prime ministers. The negative portrayal of black men is seen and interpreted as part of the racism they have faced particularly in the New World over the last five hundred years.

The purpose of this study is to probe the situation of black men in America and the Caribbean and in particular to uncover the causes of the marginalization of so many black males in these societies. The description outlined above concentrates on symptoms and manifestations readily verified by the most casual observer. It highlights the pain of those experiencing the changes and the frustration and bewilderment of those observing the situation. It is necessary to go beyond the pain and the frustration and to pinpoint the causes. This study seeks to go below the surface in order to discover why black men are overrepresented among the victims of the fallout of fundamental restructuring of New World societies in the latter part of the twentieth century. It also seeks to break new ground in the theoretical formulation and understanding of societies generally.

United States and Caribbean Comparisons

In the United States the situation of black men is often blamed on pathologies within the black community suggesting that Blacks are the causes of the problems being experienced. Blacks, on the other hand, point to systemic racism and assert that Whites must bear collective responsibility for the plight of Blacks. In the Caribbean racial lines are blurred, as in most countries, hence explanations cannot be proposed in such clear-cut and unequivocal racial terms without indulging in absurd oversimplification of the complexities involved. Moreover, race is defined differently in the two types of societies.

American and Caribbean Definitions of Race

American society defines race in term of genotype and genealogy, disregarding in many instances the physical appearance of the person. If the person has one sixty-fourth part black ancestry, he/she is defined as *black* regardless of that person's physical appearance. This conception of race highlights biological inheritance and differentiates between people on this basis. Also endemic to this genetic conception of race are assumptions of superiority and its converse, inferiority, of different racial groups.

Caribbean societies define race in terms of phenotype, the person's physical appearance, and pay little attention to genotype. *Black* and *white* are used to refer to physical appearance. This opens the possibility of intermediate categories such as *fair* and *brown*, and of different offspring of the same parents, same genotype, being classified differently. In subtle ways the phenotypic definition of race emphasizes its social construction since it highlights appearance and the social treatment accorded that appearance.

While race is conceived as discrete and dichotomous in America, it is perceived as a continuum in the Caribbean. One race can blend into another in the Caribbean. Caribbean societies are famous for their pigmentocracy which accords social meaning to shades of skin colour ranging from white at one extreme to black at the other, with brown and sambo in between. In America, racial groups are discrete and distinct.

To use the term *race* across American and Caribbean societies is to require some tolerance in the interpretation of meaning. For example, the term *Hispanic* has no racial meaning in the Caribbean because it is understood that people of Spanish culture will vary in colour just as those of other cultural roots. However, Hispanics are perceived and officially recognized as a race in America despite Caribbean skepticism about such a perception.

These differences in definition and conception of race and colour between American and Caribbean societies are highlighted to make the point that in this study race and colour are treated very much like the chemist's use of litmus paper. That is, race and colour are treated as heuristic and not analytical or objective categories. They allow the observer to see the reaction more clearly by colour coding the changes, but are not themselves the causal agents of the changes.

In other words, whatever are the factors affecting and afflicting black men in society, they are not explained solely or mainly in terms of race or racism. At best race and racism are contextual factors. By themselves they cannot explain or account for the phenomenon being described but they can make the situation worse.

Majority and Minority Groups in Societies

What is most interesting is that the description of the black man given above is more or less applicable both in the United States and the Caribbean. While there may be degrees of difference as one goes from country to country, the general scenario holds up in all countries. Significant numbers of black males are marginalized in the various societies.

One big difference between Caribbean and American society is the reversal of the numerical position of Whites and Blacks. In the United States Blacks are a minority and Whites the majority, while in the Caribbean the situation is reversed. Majority and minority speak to the question of numbers. However, the position of any group in society is not merely a question of numbers. While there are some differences between being part of a majority group and being part of a minority group in society, the numerical position of the group may be overridden by several more important considerations and factors.

The similarity of the position of Blacks in the United States and the Caribbean is that historically they have both been marginal groups in the two sets of societies. In the USA Blacks are a marginal minority, while in the Caribbean Blacks comprise marginal majorities. Likewise in America, Whites are a dominant majority; in the Caribbean they are part of dominant minorities.

It is important to give some definition of marginality and dominance at this stage. By *marginal* is meant not being holders of the reins of power in society; possessing little of the wealth of the society; generally being regarded as inferior in social status; having a belief system which justifies domination by others; and having one's position in society perpetuated by routinized relationships with others. By *dominant* is meant holding the reins of power; possessing most of the wealth; being generally regarded as superior in social status; having a belief system which justifies domination of others and having that position perpetuated by the routinized relations with others.

Caribbean and American Blacks tend to view themselves as being different. The latter pride themselves as Americans, citizens of the most wealthy and powerful country in the contemporary world and, as African-Americans, assume some superiority over their Caribbean peers who belong to marginal countries in current geopolitics. Caribbean Blacks take pride that they are part of a majority group in countries that have gained political independence. They also take pride in having made successful assaults on political power in their respective societies.

Notwithstanding these differences, Caribbean and American Blacks remain largely marginalized in their respective societies. The historical marginalization of Blacks in American and Caribbean societies can be traced back to their common experience of slavery in the New World. While slavery was abolished in the 1830s in the Caribbean and the 1860s in the United States, Blacks in both cases were forced because of limited circumstances, to remain within the ambit of the plantation on which they were enslaved. While the course of their history, in the latter part of the last century and early part of this century, varies in significant ways, both groups made the most substantial socioeconomic progress in their history in the post World War II period.

In the Caribbean this socioeconomic progress has come within the context of constitutional changes leading to adult suffrage in the 1940s and political independence in the 1960s and 1970s. In the United States similar socioeconomic progress has come within the context of the Civil Rights movement of the 1950s and 1960s. The postwar history of Blacks in America and the Caribbean is that different circumstances have led to their increasing integration into the mainstream of their respective societies. At least, the opportunities to make such advances have been greater than at any other time of their history in the New World.

The critical consideration here is, why has there been such marked differences in the social progress of black men and women, in America and the Caribbean, during the period when Blacks have made the greatest socioeconomic progress in their history in the New World? In other words, why should such gender difference arise in circumstances of integration and general socioeconomic advancement?

The context in which these differences have arisen casts doubt on explanations which put primary emphasis on slavery and its legacy among Blacks in the New World. These differences have come into full flower over one hundred years after slavery ended. While slavery would have left several social legacies and latent forms, it is difficult to understand how such latent factors could become operative without some contemporary dynamic factors playing a critical part. The question then becomes, what are these critical factors?

Current Explanations

There are several explanations currently offered for the phenomenon being described here. These explanations will be listed and briefly described below.

A Peculiar Black Phenomenon Originating in African Traditions

Herskovits (1941) proposes that the matrifocal forms noted among Blacks and the under-achievement among black men are legacies of strong matriarchal African cultural traditions that continue to survive among Blacks. The essence of this explanation is that the patterns of male marginalization observed among Blacks are peculiar to them and have their origins in African culture. The difficulty with this explanation is that it is virtually impossible to trace such traditions and patterns in Africa itself.

Certainly in contemporary West and Central Africa, from which most of the slaves came, boys have always performed and continue to perform better than girls in school, men have always dominated and continue to dominate in all positions in the labour force and men have always been and continue to be the heads of households. Why, therefore, do such very opposite patterns prevail in Africa, compared with America and the Caribbean, if these patterns originated there?

Miller (1991) has shown that male marginalization patterns similar to those manifest among Blacks are developing among Hispanics, native Americans and poorer Whites in the United States, Slavs in Russia and among some East Indians in Trinidad and Guyana. Surely male marginalization patterns emerging among these groups could not be explained in terms of African cultural survivals. Since patterns of male marginalization are found among different ethnic groups in different parts of the world, the phenomenon among Blacks cannot be explained as a unique phenomenon that is peculiar to Blacks nor can this be restricted to survivals from African culture.

Racism and Racial Discrimination in the New World

In this explanation the assertion is that Whites, who have largely constituted the ruling élites in New World societies, have historically exploited the other racial groups, particularly Blacks. Further, Whites have created their wealth by exploiting the labour of black men and by discriminating against them in such ways as to ensure their continued subordination in society. The marginalization of black males observed is therefore an outcome of racism and racial discrimination.

While there can be no gainsaying the fact that racism and racial discrimination are contexts in which black male marginalization has manifested itself, it is not at all clear that racism or racial discrimination are the primary causes. For example, in Russia male marginalization among Slavs has arisen in circumstances in which other Slavic men enjoyed the highest political and economic status, had their position in the society legitimized by the prevailing ideology and perpetuated by routinized relationships that became part of the culture. Similarly in the Caribbean, black male marginalization has continued apace, notwithstanding the rise of some black men to important positions of power, especially in the State machineries, as both bureaucrats and policy makers.

Since male marginalization can and does exist within circumstances of White against White and Black against Black, one cannot attribute racism in White against Black contests for position in society as the primary cause of the male marginalization. Racism and racial discrimination are at best contextual explanations limited to particular times and places, which conceal more fundamental primary causes.

Lack of Role Models, Ambition and a Sense of Responsibility

A very popular explanation that is often heard in many debates and discussions of the phenomenon, is that young black men lack positive role models to inspire them and on whom they could pattern their own lives. The absence of fathers in the homes, the low proportion of male teachers in the schools, and the virtual absence of men in the churches means that positive male figures are absent in the primary socializing institutions that shape the lives of the young. On the other hand, the flashy lifestyles of drug pushers, posse members and gang leaders, readily seen on the street corners, are the ones that make a powerful impact on the imagination of young black men. Surrounded by negative and deviant examples, they go astray.

Another assertion of this explanation is that black men have created their own debased situation by their lack of ambition, drive and sense of responsibility. They have done it to themselves; they have no one else to blame.

The difficulty with this explanation is that it provides no basis for understanding how black men came to the position of having very few positive role models or why negative role models predominate. Likewise, it fails to account for the lack of drive, ambition and a sense of responsibility among black men. What has led to this debased condition of black men? This explanation is singularly lacking in providing answers to this question.

The Deskilling of Labour by Capitalists

A most ingenious explanation is offered by Braverman (1979). In his *Labor and Monopoly Capital: The Degradation of Work in the Twentieth Century,* Braverman sets out a very provocative and plausible explanation of the processes by which capitalism has caused gender changes in society. Braverman's major propositions are:

(a) women constitute a long term reserve pool of labour which is now being brought into employment by the development of capitalism;
(b) there is progressive deskilling of jobs in monopoly capitalism and women take most of the new less skilled jobs; and
(c) as household tasks shift to the factory, reducing the labour to be done in the home, more women are released for work in the labour force.

According to Braverman, capitalists are continuously engaged in the progressive deskilling of jobs in order to increase their profits at the expense of their workforce. Deskilling is designed to remove control of the labour process from the skilled worker to the capitalist, by removing the conception of the task from its execution. It is also designed to reduce costs since less skilled and cheaper labour can be employed for the tasks which are of simpler execution. Women, especially those just entering the labour force, are the main source of cheap labour.

Braverman maintains that the amount of housework has decreased as a result of the increased quantity of household goods that are available from the market-place. Clothing and pre-prepared foodstuffs are some of the items that can be produced cheaper under the capitalist relations and forces of production than under domestic ones. This releases women from domestic chores and facilitates their availability for wage labour.

These two parallel processes promote the movement of women into the workforce, from the reserve pool of labour, into new deskilled jobs in offices and factories. Thus women's participation rates in the labour market have been increasing at the same time that the participation rates for men have been declining as they are pushed out from skilled labour, become unemployed or retire early. These changes in participation rates of men and women in the labour force, have implications for family patterns, gender relations and by implication the increasing marginalization of men, including black men.

If Braverman's very ingenious and plausible explanation is indeed valid, then one would expect that the industrialized Western capitalist economies of the United States, Canada and Western Europe would have the highest level of female participation in the labour force. Also, up to 1990, the Soviet Union and other Eastern bloc countries operated centrally planned economies that virtually eliminated the profit motive and that, as a consequence, produced very few domestic goods by industrial means that relieved women of their domestic chores. If Braverman's explanation is valid, then Eastern bloc command economies should have relatively low participation rates of females in the labour force compared to Western capitalist economies. Table 1.1 shows comparisons of the proportion of women participating in the labour force in different types of economies between 1950 and 1985.

Table 1.1 Proportion of Women in the Labour Force

Types of Countries	1950	1975	1985
Centrally planned industrialized	48	48	47
Industrialized market economies	30	36	38
Latin American and Caribbean	18	24	27
Asia and Oceana	39	42	43
Africa	42	41	39

Source: Women in the World of Work, ILO (1989).

Table 1.1 shows that over the period 1950 to 1985 the centrally planned industrialized economies had the highest proportion of women in the economically active population in the labour force of all the types of countries and economies in the world. The industrialized market economies had much lower rates of participation of women in the workforce. Indeed, only Latin American and Caribbean economies had lower rates of female labour force participation than the industrialized market economies.

First, the Soviet Union and other formerly centrally planned economies, in which market forces and employers acting on the basis of profit maximization were absent, brought a larger proportion of women into the labour force working full-time, than all capitalist market economies.

Secondly, deskilling of jobs by employers (for the purpose of profit maximization at the expense of the workforce) by their employing women in place of the men displaced did not happen in the Soviet Union. Indeed, several aspects of the Soviet economy remained labour intensive. The pace of technological development in the Soviet Union was slower than in Western countries, particularly in the production of consumer goods.

Thirdly, women's entry into the labour force in the Soviet Union took place in spite of the fact that industrial production has not replaced domestic production to any significant degree. On the contrary, the prospect of using industrial methods to produce domestic goods and services is a dream Soviet women now embrace to relieve them ultimately of much of the burden of their domestic chores. The Soviet experience shows that while industrial production of domestic goods and services can be supportive of women's increased participation in the labour force, it is not the cause. While such production can make it easier for women to participate in the labour force, it is not a necessary condition for such participation to take place in the first instance.

Braverman's ingenious explanation, which appears very plausible, does not receive any empirical support in one of the most successful instances of the involvement of women in the workforce of any country or type of economy. One can only conclude that women's participation in the labour force and the gender segregation that is commonly observed are not unique manifestations of a capitalist economy. Other unidentified causal processes are operative in both capitalist market and socialist command economies. The deskilling of labour by the capitalist for increased profit is at best a contextual explanation which cannot be generalized.

OUTLINING AN ALTERNATIVE EXPLANATION

None of the explanations cited above can satisfactorily account for the complexity of the phenomenon of marginalization of the black male. The assertion that this is a phenomenon peculiar and unique to Blacks arising from African traditions cannot be sustained by either historical or sociological evidence. While racism and racial discrimination are certainly factors in some of the contexts in which male marginalization is observed to occur, they are certainly not the causal factors. The popular perception that the problem is mainly socio/psychological resulting from the absence of appropriate male role models in schools and homes is simplistic and misses the point that the phenomenon being examined is centred around the changing role of men and women in society. The issue is not the absence of models of the role but changes in the traditional roles themselves. Braverman's intriguingly ingenious and very plausible theory is contradicted by the available empirical evidence.

The challenge is, therefore, to propose an explanation that can accommodate the complexity of the phenomenon being observed and which also accords with the evidence. One important point on which there is agreement with Braverman is that gender changes in society have to be understood and interpreted in relationship to broader structural changes that are occurring in society. The disagreement with Braverman is with respect to the particular structures to which he relates the changes.

From the perspective of this study, labour and capital are not the most critical and important considerations. Rather, the critical factors are the relative positions of groups in society; their differences in the degree to which they control access to opportunities of upward mobility; their contest and competition for position in society; and the mechanisms employed to settle these questions as they are played out at different times in history.

The Theory of Place

Miller (1990) postulated the theory of place in which he asserted that society was organized on the basis of place: the relative positions and relationships of individuals and groups with respect to power, resources, status, belief, and culture. Place is a unitary entity comprised of the five dimensions noted. Hence no aspect of society could be understood solely in terms of power, resources, status, belief, or culture although one dimension may contribute more than the others to a particular aspect of society at any particular time.

According to this theory an egalitarian society is a utopian ideal that can never be achieved in reality because all individuals or groups in society cannot have the same relations relative to each other with respect to power, resources, status, belief, and culture unless some restrictions are put on the definition of all, or individuals, or groups. Relative inequality is the reality of society. Places in society are therefore scattered between centre and margin. At any particular moment in time some individuals and groups in society will be more central and others more marginal.

The real dilemma in human society, however, is that the relative inequality which is the reality cannot be absolutely or permanently justified. In other words, the relative inequality which is the reality in society is inherently arbitrary and unjust. The continuing and persistent dialectic in society is that the egalitarian ideal which is inherently just is a practical impossibility, while the relative inequality which is the practical reality is inherently arbitrary and unjust.

However, society and community cannot operate without structure, that is, some basis on which to justify or allocate inequality. According to the theory of place, societies invariably invent criteria which are used to allocate place and to arbitrate dissension related to inequality. These criteria can be regarded as operational absolutes in that they are put forward as if they were the only right and rational basis for determining the relative relations of individuals and groups in society, while at the same time they are no more than the operational basis on which the dilemma of inequality in society is addressed in that specific period of the society's history. In other words, the injustice and arbitrary nature of these operational absolutes are eventually highlighted and contested and may or may not lead to their eventual removal or modification.

Accordingly, over the long haul of history, place in society is being forever contested and the basis of societal organization is perennially being challenged. The basis of rationalizing inequality is repeatedly renegotiated. While there may be periods marked by consensus concerning the operational absolutes employed, these periods are invariably followed by conflict and challenge of the criteria used to temporarily abate the issues of inequality and injustice in society.

From the perspective of the theory of place, the structure of society, at any particular time, is determined by the combination and interaction of the operational absolutes being employed by a society in that period of its history. In other words, the operational absolutes determine the place structure of the society and these are reflected in all the power, resource, status, belief, and cultural relationships in the society.

Application of the Theory of Place to the Study of Gender

In applying the theory of place to the study of gender in any society the critical questions to be posed are: (1) What are the operational absolutes employed by the particular society in allocating place? (2) If gender is one of the criteria, how does it operate in conjunction with the others?

Let us suppose that a society at some time in the past employed length of toes, gender and age as the operational absolutes by which places were allocated and justified in that society. Let us also assume that long toes were preferred over short toes, that male was preferred over female and that older was preferred over younger. Further, let us assume that length of toe is the primary operational absolute, while gender and age are the secondary and tertiary absolutes, respectively.

According to the theory, places in that society would be distributed unequally, that is from centre to margin, based on the combination and interactions of these three operational absolutes. Figure 1.1 below shows the place structure and queue that would result from the interaction of these operational absolutes.

Figure 1.1 Toe Length Patriarchy

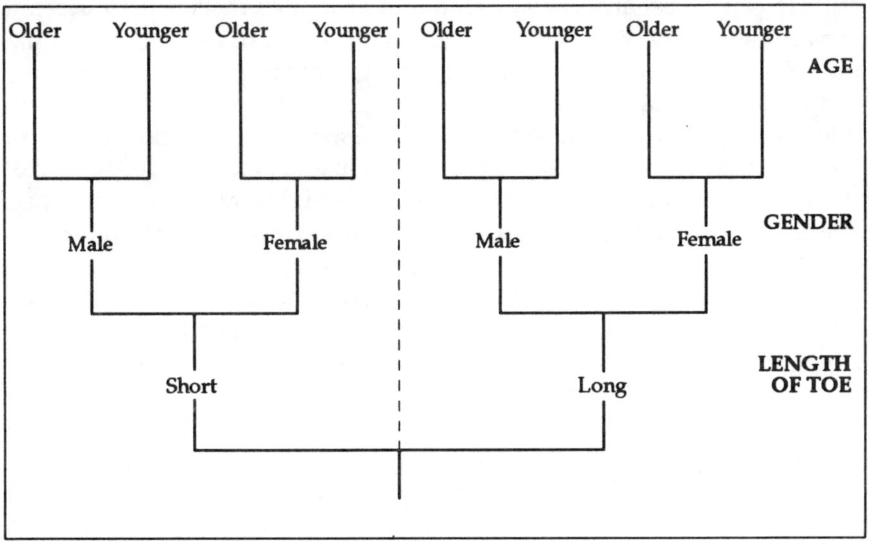

It can be seen from Figure 1.1 that in this society older long-toe men would occupy the most central places and would be at the head of the queue, while younger short-toe females would be most marginalized and would be located at the end of the queue. Between these two extremes would be groups of persons marginalized or centralized on the basis of one or two of the operational absolutes. For example, younger long-toe males would be marginalized with respect to age but centralized with respect to maleness and toes. Likewise, older long-toe females would be centralized with respect to age and toe but marginalized with respect to femaleness. Younger short-toe males would be centralized with respect to maleness but marginalized with respect to age and toe.

The central position of older long-toe males would be reflected in the fact that they would exercise the most power and influence, possess the greatest amount of wealth, display the most luxurious lifestyle, enjoy the highest social regard and esteem, have their position justified and legitimized by the belief system and prevailing ideology and perpetuated by the routinized relationships and outlooks embedded in the culture.

Younger short-toe females who are triply marginalized, as short toe, female and young, will have their position reflected in all the power, resource, status, belief and cultural relations in the society. Hence the marginality of these females will be reflected in the fact that they will have the least power and influence, struggle to secure the basic means of survival, be regarded as inferior, have the belief system and prevailing ideology justify their triple marginality and have their peripheral position perpetuated by the routinized relations embedded in the culture.

Special note should be taken of three intermediary groups in the place queue: younger long-toe men, older long-toe women and older short-toe men. These groups are each only marginal on one operational absolute: age, gender and toe, respectively. These groups would potentially pose the greatest threat to the hegemony of the older long-toe men. The threat of the younger long-toe men is mediated by the prospect of succession. In time they will become the older long-toe men occupying the head of the queue. It is in the interest of young long-toe men to wait their turn since this preserves the operational absolutes on which the queue is based. Also, it is in the interest of the older long-toe men to groom these younger men who will succeed them, since this will reassure the younger men and help forestall any challenge from them.

The circumstances of the older long-toe women are somewhat different. To permit their free upward movement in the queue would compromise the gender operational absolute on which the queue is based. Such movement would therefore only be permitted in exceptional circumstances where there were no old or young long-toe men to move into those places and would be restricted only to such women who could be trusted not to further undermine or compromise the operational absolutes on which the place structure of the society is predicated.

The case of the older short-toe men is of particular interest. To permit their free upward movement in the queue would be to compromise the most fundamental of the operational absolutes, length of toe. Very few such men therefore would be allowed upward movement in the queue. However, because the older short-toe men occupy the highest position in the queue of the short-toe group, within that group they would exercise a certain hegemony over the entire short-toe group. Their position in the short-toe group would be reinforced if the society was segregated based on length of toe since this group would exercise control of some institutions within short-toe communities.

According to the theory of place, this structure would be reflected generally in all social institutions within the society as well as in all power, resource, status, belief and cultural relations. However, the exact manner in which the general place structure and queue exert their impact on the various institutions of society will vary according to the institutions and the contextual factors relative to the operations of those institutions. For example, while the place queue may be reflected almost exactly in the access of the various groups to education and to the quality and quantity of education they receive, the labour market queue may be different in that long-toe women, particularly the older women may be absent from the workforce. The exact relationships existing between the general place structure and specific institutions one wished to study, would therefore need to be established empirically and contextually.

A society so structured on the basis of toes, gender and age could be described as a toe length patriarchal society. Older long-toe men would be the supreme patriarchs exercising hegemony over all groups in the society. At the same time, older short-toe men, while being limited in their power, status and wealth, would exercise some hegemony over younger short-toe men and older and younger short-toe women.

It is important to note that as long as there is no challenge of the operational absolutes from any group within the society, toe length patriarchy is preserved. The traditional place structure of the society would remain unchanged and the relative importance of each absolute remains undisturbed. According to the theory of place, because the operational absolutes are inherently unjust and cannot permanently or absolutely justify inequality in society, there will come the time when the short-toe group will begin to challenge toe length as a just basis on which to structure society. That is, they will contest the notion that length of toe is a fair and just basis on which to allocate place in the society.

According to the theory the outcome of any particular challenge cannot be guaranteed. Changes in the place structure are not linear. However, over time challenges may lead to changes in the operational absolutes on which the society is structured. Also challenge to one criterion of social organization can have implications for the other criteria on which the place structure is predicated.

For the sake of illustration, let us assume that in the circumstances of the challenge by the short-toe group it is not feasible for the long-toe group to squash the short-toe group by the use of naked force. That is, they are not able, for one reason or another, to physically eliminate the short-toe group totally or partially. Neither are they able to ignore the challenge. Let us assume that for a concatenation of reasons the long-toe group finds itself in the position where it must respond to the challenge by conceding positions to the short-toe group thus bringing some amount of integration in the place structure. The assumption is also that the short-toe group is actively seeking integration into the mainstream of the society.

What can also be assumed is that on the whole the majority of persons, of both groups, will act to preserve or enhance their place and that of their group in the society. That is, most members of the society will be actors in the contest for place in society. In the main, most individuals and groups will act rationally and intentionally, within the calculus of advantage determined by the operational absolutes, and in so doing seek their own best interest and that of their group. Within this framework it is possible to predict the likely steps that will be taken by the different groups in the context of the circumstances outlined above.

Given the prevailing toe length patriarchy that obtains in the society, it would be expected that the challenge from the short-toe group would be led by the men of that group and that it would be focused on the men of the long-toe group. In other words while the women of both groups would be involved, the men will be the principal actors and would be mostly in the limelight.

Some of the actions that can be expected to be taken by the various groups consequent upon the challenge and the outcomes of these actions can be summarized and listed briefly as follows:

(a) The long-toe men can be expected to act in such a manner as to protect the central position of the long-toe group and in particular that of long-toe men, old and young. They therefore could be expected to concede immediately very limited opportunities to old short-toe men and only slightly more to younger short-toe men. The concessions would largely be token: limited immediate action promising more substantial changes in the future. Limited and token though such concessions would be, they would result in several young short-toe men not only succeeding their fathers but exceeding them in the place structure.

(b) Because the position of long-toe women would be most compromised by the concessions to the short-toe men, it can be expected that they would seek to regain the real or perceived loss of position in the place structure. The long-toe women could be expected to be focused on their disadvantage in society as women and to contrast their continued marginalization with the recent enfranchisement accorded to short-toe men. Long-toe men could therefore concede some opportunities to women in some institutions of society depending on the intensity of the challenge from the short-toe group and from the long-toe women.

(c) Faced with the twin challenges from the short-toe group and long-toe women, over time, long-toe men can be expected to concede most of the opportunities to younger short-toe females. By so doing they would be responding to the challenges from both the short-toe group and from their women. By conceding most of the opportunities to the most marginalized in the society, long-toe men would be taking a line of action that would allow them the greatest chance of and flexibility in withstanding and containing the challenges from both quarters. Consequently, in time, many young short-toe females will exceed their brothers, mothers and fathers in their upward mobility in the society.

(d) One outcome of the strategic response of the long-toe men would be to increase inequality between men in the society as their places become polarized at the two ends of the queue, at the top and bottom of the place hierarchy. On the other hand, women's relative positions in the society would become more equalized as they become more concentrated in the middle of the queue.

(e) Another outcome would be a ceiling erected and maintained to restrict the level to which women could rise in the queue. Certainly that ceiling would generally be below that of the younger long-toe men or in extreme circumstance just lower than that of the older long-toe men. In other words all women in the society would have great difficulty in succeeding to positions at the head of the queue, except in very unusual circumstances.

(f) A further outcome would be the emergence of matrifocal forms in the short-toe group as a result of younger women being skipped in the place queue. These patterns would emerge in all the social institutions in which the short-toe group participated and over which the long-toe group exercised control. Short-toe patriarchy would be undermined in numerous ways. The impact of this would be to shift the socializing patterns among the short-toe group from favouring their boys to favouring their girls. The short-toe group would be participants in this shift since it represents the principal means by which the group is able to access the opportunities resulting from the challenge of the place structure of the society.

(g) The most far-reaching consequence of the concessions made, however, is the compromise of the operational absolutes on which place in the society is based. By advancing younger women over older men and older women, age is compromised; by advancing younger women over their brothers and fathers, gender is compromised; and by equalizing the position of long and short-toe women, length of toe is compromised. The result is paradox and contradiction in the place structure and in most of the dimensions of place.

(h) The direction of the society, faced with these contradictions in the place structure, cannot be guaranteed. Toe length patriarchy could be reinstated by force. The short-toe group could reverse its position in the society by seizing the central places. Toe length could be replaced by a new criterion, width of toe, which may preserve some aspects of the status quo while permitting change within a new place structure. Because human society is open-ended, the future course of any society is the outcome of the prior choices made by the contending parties and the dynamics of their interaction in the contemporary situation.

One point that needs to be noted from the above analysis is that once any marginalized group in society begins to contest its position in the place structure, it is possible that a chain reaction could be set in motion as other marginalized groups are spurred into action by the perceived or real changes that result or could result from the challenges posed. This could trigger a state of flux in the society as the old place structure is deemed outmoded without the emergence of a new and uncontested structure.

While the eventual outcome would be uncertain, the possibilities are almost unlimited. Young long-toe men could seize the central places from the older generation. Long and short-toe men could unite to continue to marginalize women. That is, gender could be elevated to being the primary operational absolute in the place structure, and women could unite to seize the central places – that is, reversing their position relative to men. The short-toe group could seize the central places and marginalize the long-toe group. Short-toe women could hold most of the central positions by virtue of their greater expertise, experience and exposure during the period of sponsored mobility when the long-toe group opened up opportunities in the society.

The critical factors determining the eventual outcomes will be the coalitions formed by the various groups in pursuit of their place-interests, self-determination, and the length of time over which these interactions between the coalitions operate. Shorter time would favour coalitions involving groups holding power or those close to power; longer time would favour coalitions involving the more marginal groups.

TESTING THE THEORY

Whether a society responding to internal challenges to its basis of organization will adopt new operational absolutes or reinstate the old ones depends on numerous factors outside the scope of this study. The focus here is to ascertain whether there is empirical and historical evidence to support the theory of place as it is applied to gender changes in society. If the theory is to be useful it must be more than plausible, it must accord with reality as verified by empirical findings and historical experience. Also, it must be a more economical and meaningful way of handling the bewildering array of facts, observations and findings relative to the issues being examined.

The assertion here is that the situation of Blacks in American and Caribbean societies is very analogous to the short-toe group cited in the hypothetical example of the application of the theory. The difference is that the real situation will be far more complex than the hypothetical example. To test the theory it is necessary to select a society and apply the tenets of place theory to that society. Jamaica was the society chosen for the purpose of testing the theory. The choice of Jamaica was largely one of convenience and not due to any special considerations.

An analysis will therefore be done of gender changes in the Jamaican society. In essence this will be a case study to give some initial indication of the power of the theory of place to explain gender changes that have defied satisfactory answers from other approaches.

Operational Absolutes in the Jamaican Society

The first order of business in testing the theory in this case study is to identify the groups that have composed the Jamaican society and the operational absolutes on which the society was originally structured. By so doing it should be possible to establish the traditional place structure and place queue, as these relate to the groups that originally composed the society. From that starting point it should be possible to trace the changes, if any, that have occurred.

Modern Jamaican society traces its origin to the British conquest of the island in 1655. The groups that composed the society were Whites, Jews, Blacks and Mulattoes, the latter named group being the offspring of the white and black unions or liaisons. The society practised slavery and bond service, hence within each group there were subgroups. Probably the concept of status groups would be the most appropriate to describe the subcategories within each racial group. All groups had more men than women.

The operational absolutes on which the society was organized could be identified as race, status groups, gender and age. However, the institution of slavery imposed many distortions and convolutions in the place structure. For the purpose of this study it is meaningful to commence the analysis of the place structure following Emancipation when many of the distortions and convolutions were officially removed.

Institutions Offering Upward Social Mobility to Blacks

Another important element in testing the theory in this case study is to identify institutions that have offered upward social mobility to Blacks in the Jamaican society since Emancipation. The validity of the theory and support for its premises will depend on the nature of the gender changes, if any, that have occurred in these institutions.

The occupations open to Blacks immediately after Emancipation were the same as those that were available to them during slavery: artisan trades, agricultural labour, petty trading and domestic service. The only new occupation that became open to them was elementary school teaching following the inauguration of an elementary school system designed almost exclusively to cater to children of ex-slaves. This system of mass education was established as part of the infrastructure that should support and maintain the newly created free society.

Elementary school teaching as an occupation became accessible to Blacks for four main reasons. First, their children were the vast majority of the pupils attending the public elementary schools. Secondly, the system was owned and managed by the churches of which they were members and by reason of which they had some say in determining the general structure of the system. Thirdly, the system was fee-paying and as the major clients they had considerable influence in setting curriculum, admission and employment policies. Fourthly, the financial structure of the elementary school system only allowed it to import large numbers of expatriate teachers for the first decade of its existence, 1834 to 1844. After this first decade almost all teachers were recruited locally.

Given these circumstances and the fact that Blacks were important stakeholders in the denominational system of mass elementary education that was established immediately after Emancipation, it is not surprising that public elementary school teaching became a "black occupation" in Jamaica after 1846.

From the outset of the creation of the elementary school system it was accepted by the various denominations that they had to make provision for the training of teachers. Several denominations and one interdenominational group, Mico, established teachers' colleges. Given the structure of the elementary school system and the elementary school teaching occupation that emerged, it was only natural that Blacks gained access to teachers' colleges.

Interestingly the teachers' college became their only prospect of receiving education beyond the elementary level, as apart from training teachers, these colleges became the secondary schools and colleges for Blacks.

Following Emancipation, elementary school teaching thus became the first professional occupation that was open to Blacks. As such it became the focal point of their occupational mobility. Likewise, teachers' colleges were their only route of educational advancement leading to occupational mobility. These colleges therefore became the centrepiece of the educational attainment of Blacks and a focal point of their ambition and striving.

These two related institutions offering upward social mobility to Blacks have operated continuously for more than one hundred and fifty years. They are therefore prime social institutions in which to study gender changes related to Blacks and therefore for testing the theory.

No claim is being made here that Blacks in Jamaica have only had educational and occupational mobility through elementary school teaching and teachers' colleges. Certainly they have gained access to theological education and had access to occupational mobility through the clergy. Also, in more recent times, they have gained access to high school and university education and through these to practically all the white-collar and professional occupations in the labour force. The point is that advances made through these educational institutions and occupation are later developments. Additionally, in many instances, these more recent advancements were related to initial opportunities accessed through elementary school teaching and teachers' colleges.

Black Challenges to the Status Quo

The final step in testing the theory in this case study is to identify periods in the Jamaican society, since Emancipation in 1838, when Blacks challenged the traditional place structure and demanded a fairer distribution of opportunities. Three such periods can be identified: the Morant Bay Rebellion of 1865, the 1938 riots, and the Black Power movement of the late 1960s.

The focus of the case study must therefore be on the gender patterns that were established in teachers' colleges and elementary school teaching following Emancipation and prior to the Morant Bay

Rebellion; the changes that occurred after 1865; the changes that occurred after 1938; and those which have occurred in the last twenty years.

METHODOLOGY

The methodology of the study can be conveniently outlined in three steps. First, the place structure of the Jamaican society is derived, given the groups that composed the society and the operational absolutes previously identified. The structure and governance of the elementary school system is then related to the place structure and the changes over time in the light of challenges from Blacks and responses from the ruling central groups.

Secondly, empirical data were collected from official sources concerning the institutional provisions for elementary schools and teachers' colleges; the gender composition of elementary school teachers and principals; and the enrolment, by gender, in teachers' colleges. Strenuous efforts were made to collect these data for the 150-year period under review. Some data are also reported on high school and university enrolment, by gender, especially in periods when Blacks began to gain access to these institutions in appreciable numbers.

Thirdly, an analysis was done of the sociological, economic and political factors that appear to be related to any shifts in gender found in the empirical data. This analysis draws upon studies done in these fields which elucidate the issues being studied.

From the synthesis of the results of these three elements of the methodology, suitable inferences are drawn concerning the questions for which answers are sought. From this process attempts are made to determine the extent to which the theory of place provides satisfying answers to the question of the marginalization of black males in Jamaican society.

2

THE THEORY OF PLACE AND JAMAICAN MALE MARGINALIZATION

Before proceeding to the substance of this chapter, it is necessary to make some introductory remarks on the subjects of race, class, gender, and age. No one can deny the reality of race, class, gender, and age as bases on which Caribbean, including Jamaican, societies have been organized historically. Both the lived experiences of the people and empirical research attest to their reality. Mills (1993) called race, class and gender "a kind of unholy trinity – the three main axes of social differentiation, the three main dimensions of social oppression". Age is often ignored in discussions of social organization, although generation is a potent factor in shaping the lives of people and the nature of social institutions.

The contentious issues related to race, class, gender, and age are raised not with respect to their reality in society, but with respect to their conceptualization and formulation in social theory. The currently entrenched social theories all seem to have serious shortcomings in dealing with the totality represented by race, class, gender, and age in society.

Marxism asserts the primacy of class, people's ranked relationship to the means of production. Accordingly, all social structures in society have their origin in the exploitation of labour by capital and the mechanisms of that exploitation. All racial conflicts, according to classical Marxism, can be reduced to class conflicts given the primacy of economic factors. But if this is so, why then are there variations in the upward mobility of persons of different races who have the same ranked position to the means of production? Yet, such variations are often found in empirical studies. For example, Gordon (1991), using a Marxist definition of class, showed that in the postwar period light-skinned lower class Jamaicans enjoyed much higher rates of upward inter-generational mobility than their dark-skinned peers.

Weberian functionalism defines class largely in terms of market opportunities or life chances and prestige or consumption differences between groups. Race is conceptualized as the closure of economic opportunities by one group against another; hence, like Marxism, racial conflicts and differences can be reduced to class and status group conflicts and differences. But, Weberian theory makes no differentiation between the life chances or prestige of men and women of the same class, race, or status groups. However, empirical studies abound that show that women of the same technical expertise, competence, experience, and consumption patterns in the marketplace often are paid less and enjoy much less prestige than their male peers. Why should gender make any difference in the marketplace if individuals are valued and rewarded on the basis of their functional contribution?

Dev (1985) makes the point that existing social theories, including functionalism, are uniformly unisex in that they make no differentiation between men and women and often assume that women's status or class is dependent upon and derived from males. In other words, conventional and radical theories that attempt to address issues of race and class have ignored gender.

Feminist scholars noting the limitations of existing social theories concerning gender, have been developing theories of patriarchy. While there is so far no comprehensive and widely accepted theory of patriarchy, attempts have been made to address the issues of class, gender, and age—for example, Hartman (1979 and 1981). However, Walby (1990) is of the opinion that Hartman's inclusion of a generational element in her conception of patriarchy introduces notions of men dominating other men. This Walby sees as a mistake because in her opinion it confuses the issue. According to Walby, theorizing concerning patriarchy should be restricted to systems of social structure and practices in which men dominate and exploit women.

But even if one were to overlook the division among feminist scholars concerning the inclusion of age as a dimension of patriarchy, it is not possible to ignore the criticism that feminist theorizing concerning patriarchy has largely ignored the issue of race, Amos and Parmar (1984) and Barrett and McIntosh (1985). In other words, while theorizing on patriarchy addresses gender issues frontally, and in the main addresses issues of class, to date it has not dealt adequately either with the issue of age or race.

The most comprehensive theory attempting to link race, class, gender, and age has been M.G. Smith's theory of cultural pluralism (Smith 1984), although its treatment of gender is somewhat weak and incidental. According to Smith, society is structured on the basis of basic and secondary institutions. A homogenous society is one in which members share in both basic and secondary institutions. A heterogeneous society is one in which members share basic institutions but diverge in their participation in secondary institutions. A plural society is one in which members do not share either basic or secondary institutions. In a plural society it is force that keeps the separate cultural sections together, and the state is little more than a committee of the dominant cultural élite and is the ultimate instrument of internal domination and the corporate control of the subject sections.

The theory of cultural pluralism identifies race or ethnicity as a major source of cultural difference in society; class as a source of variation within ethnic groups and cultural sections; and notes patriarchal and matriarchal structures in the kinship traditions among various cultural segments, thus addressing some generational and gender issues. Massiah (1987), however, points to its limitations in dealing with women's issues.

The major weaknesses in this theory, however, are in accounting for why societies are homogenous, heterogeneous or plural in the first place; the rigidity of the plural model itself; and its difficulty in accounting for evolutionary social changes in the structure of plural societies. No attempt will be made here to repeat the exhaustive critique of the theory of cultural pluralism that has raged since the early 1960s. [See Smith (1961 and 1967), Kuper (1976), Lowenthal (1972) and La Guerre (1993).]

However, one has to agree with Smith (1984) that, despite its limitations, the construct of cultural pluralism is intellectually superior to notions of race and ethnicity, class, caste, minorities, social classification and primodality as explanations by themselves. The latter constructs tend to be single dimension explanations of society, while cultural pluralism seeks to incorporate them all into an integrated system, even if it assumes the primacy of culture.

One lesson learned from Smith's work is that when theorizing about Caribbean society the theorist should be universalist and not parochial. Another lesson is that theories explaining Caribbean society can contribute much to understanding societies everywhere. Yet another lesson is that his break with conventional and radical theories in vogue in Western academies was critical to the formulation of a more comprehensive theoretical construction of race, class, gender, and age as they operate in society.

The challenge from Smith's work is not necessarily to expand or revise the plural society construct in order to overcome its shortcomings. Rather, it is to formulate social theories that are more comprehensive, less rigid and static, and more tolerant of flux in society.

Dev (1985) observed that theories dealing with socioeconomic changes constitute a weak-point of the social sciences especially where they attempt to address the issue of gender. Reddock (1993) goes further to state that theorizing about women's issues has been approached as an additive concept which competes for primacy with class. As such, gender has not been treated substantively in social theorizing. La Guerre (1993) makes the point that social theories used to explain race and class in Caribbean societies, including Smith's, have been imported and are therefore not entirely appropriate. He suggests that deeper critical assessments be made of these approaches. By implication La Guerre seems to be signalling the need for theories of Caribbean societies formulated from first principles. Mills (1993) called for theoretical innovations, given the current state of theory in the social sciences. Greene (1993) sees the prospect of reformulating the interrelationships between race, class, kinship, and gender into more integrative theory. The circumstances seem auspicious for a new theoretical venture in addressing the issues of race, class, gender, and generation in society.

Some Relevant Aspects of the Theory of Place

Before applying the theory of place to Jamaican society it is necessary to make some further reference to relevant aspects of this theory, since it is not possible to repeat a full and exhaustive exposition in this study. These observations can be summarized as follows:

1. It is the relativities in society with respect to place – that is, the intersection and integration of power, resources, status, belief, and culture – that give society its structure and dynamic. In other words, it is differential access to power and resources; differences in according honour and prestige; differences in belief that justify and legitimate action; and differences in the routinized relationships, habitual perceptions and settled outlooks that mediate structure and dynamic in society. This is so both at the micro and macro levels of social organization and social functioning.
2. Inequality in place is the reality of society. Accordingly, places scatter and cluster between centre and margin. Within the place structure of any society there will be intersection, overlap and discontinuities which readily invalidate and frustrate attempts to reduce the structure to simple categories. Social equality is a utopian ideal not realized in reality. The inequality that constitutes social reality is inherently unjust. Left without some basis for ordering inequality, society would be in continuous confusion and chaos (see page 12 et seq.).

3. Invariably, society imposes operational absolutes as the basis of mediating and justifying inequality. These operational absolutes not only become the basis of social organization but also the framework for rational action to secure and maintain place advantage. They establish the calculus of advantage and disadvantage in the society which almost everyone can use in their long- and short-term calculations. Because the operational absolutes are arbitrary and incomplete, there are always inconsistencies in the logic and rationale of the place structure they create.
4. No single actor or group of actors can contemplate all the consequences of the actions they take to secure their advantage. As a result, there are always unintended consequences to actions taken by individuals or groups to secure place advantage in society. In addition, because of the protracted nature of social change, causes and their consequences are so separated in time as to permit doubt and uncertainty concerning their connection. Again, many actors in the social arena are not forced to face the long-term consequences of their decisions.
5. Place in society is not only the result of the relative relationships between persons in that society but also the consequence of the relative relations between that society and the other societies to which it is interrelated.That is, place in society has both internal and external aspects. Place between societies is governed by the same principles as place within society. That is, there is relative inequality between societies that are inherently unjust. Operational absolutes are usually imposed to mediate and justify inequality between societies, for example, development/underdevelopment in the postwar era. These operational absolutes establish the calculus of advantage/disadvantage in inter-societal relations.
6. In contesting place within and between societies all individuals and groups act with motive and intention. All are actors. Accordingly, individuals and groups are constantly forming coalitions to secure their intentions. These coalitions may be with others in horizontal, vertical, or diagonal positions in the place structure. As a result, centrals form coalitions among themselves, with marginals and with those with intermediate positions in the place structure. Over time, coalitions form and fracture depending on the extent to which they are useful in securing the intentions of the coalition members. When coalitions fracture, the members often re-establish previous coalitions, especially because these old alliances become strong rallying points for the dissolving of the coalition.

PLACE THEORY AND THE JAMAICAN SOCIETY

In applying place theory to the Jamaican society and to this study it is necessary to establish the general place structure of Jamaica following Emancipation and also the place queue that was operative in education. The latter is the specific focus of this study in that it is teacher college enrolment and the elementary school occupation that are the principal objects of investigation.

The Place Structure of Jamaican Society

Figure 2.1 shows that the Jamaican place structure, following Emancipation, was based on three racial or colour groups, three social classes, two genders, and two age groups. Race/colour was the primary criterion, followed in rank order by class, gender, and age. Accordingly, the place structure could be said to be mainly ascriptive since it was based on three ascriptive criteria, race/colour, gender, and age. Class is employed here mainly in its Weberian definition and is therefore seen primarily as an achievement category reflecting accomplishments in occupation, education, and earnings.

The categorization of age here is most arbitrary. Probably a more appropriate classification may have been children, young adults, adults, and the old. The decision was taken that four age groups would require a degree of refinement to the analysis which is not really essential to the exercise.

Figure 2.1 General Place Structure: the Jamaican Society Following Emancipation

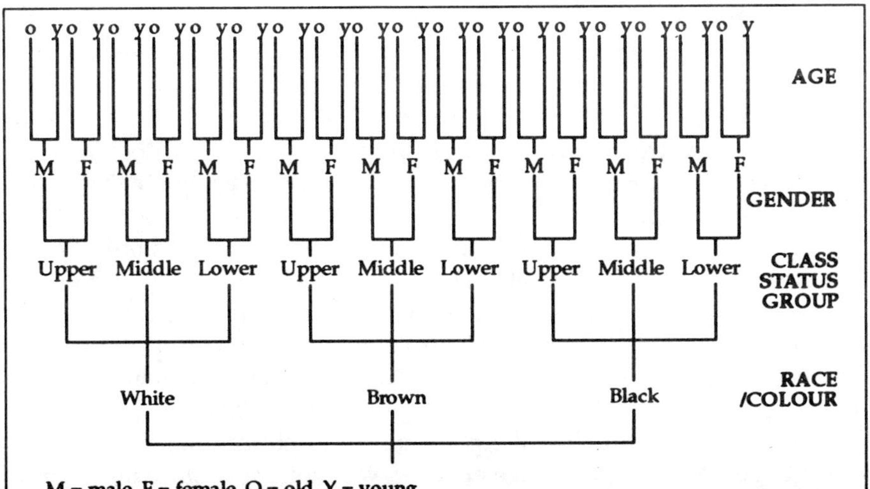

The place structure of Jamaican society following Emancipation was dominated by race/colour. This was the primary criterion of the place structure. The term "white" is used here to include all persons of European ancestry. Some were bureaucrats from Britain, planters of large and small holdings and their support staff; professionals, and those who had fallen on hard times. The term "brown" is used to include persons of mulatto heritage and Jewish ancestry. This group was accorded their civil rights in the society in the period leading up to Emancipation. The term "black" is used to include all persons of African ancestry most of whom were slaves but some were freed persons at the time of Emancipation.

Within each colour group there were status groups or classes. Differences in education, occupation and earnings differentiated the groups. However, the Whites of the lowest status groups regarded themselves and in many respects were treated as superior to Browns of the highest status groups within the brown colour group. The same could be said about the relative relations between Browns and Blacks.

Within each colour and class/status group, males were accorded higher education, occupation and earning opportunities than females. Moreover, the older persons enjoyed seniority to younger persons in gaining access to leadership, decision-making and prominent positions in the society. The place structure that existed could be labelled "colour/class patriarchy".

The Place Queue in Education

Figure 2.1, and the description above, outline the general place structure of the Jamaican society; that is, the generally ranked positions of groups, based on the operational absolutes employed to mediate and justify inequality in the society following Emancipation. However, the exact manner in which this general structure impacts upon the various institutions of the society, in any historical period, varies with the particular institution and its interrelationships with the other institutions in society.

For example, the place queue in education will not only be the product of the operational absolutes but in addition will be influenced and determined by the interaction of the education system with other social, economic, and cultural institutions in the context of the general place structure. Hence the labour market, the state machinery, and marriage could be factors influencing place in the education queue.

In seeking to establish the place queue in education several points need to be noted. First, the age criterion will not apply since only young people are involved. In nineteenth century Jamaica, formal education was restricted to the young. Secondly, the place queue in education will reflect the extent to which any group needed education to maintain or enhance their place in society. Where education would make little or no difference to place, then one could expect to find limited provision for, or limited participation in what is provided.

Table 2.1 Place Queue in Education Following Emancipation

Rank order of groups	Type of schooling/highest level attained
Segment A	
1. White upper-class male	Governess/English public/ some university
2. Brown upper-class male	Governess/some English public/ few university
3. White middle-class male	Private/trust/few university
4. White lower-class male	Private/some trust/few college
Brown middle-class male	Private/some trust/few college
Black upper-class male	Private/some trust/few college
5. White middle-class female	Private/trust/some finishing school
Brown upper-class female	Private/trust/some finishing school
6. Brown middle-class female	Private/trust
Black upper-class female	Private/trust
7. White upper-class female	Governess/finishing school
Segment B	
8. Black middle-class male	Elementary
Brown lower-class male	Elementary
9. Black lower-class male	Some elementary
Black middle-class female	Some elementary
10. White lower-class female	Little or no education
Brown lower-class female	Little or no education
Black lower-class female	Little or no education

Source: Developed from the Latrobe Report (1837) Schedule B.

To establish the education queue following Emancipation it was necessary to examine reports of the schools that existed and their chief clientele. Table 2.1 shows a rough approximation of the place queue in education that seemed operative in the Jamaican society following Emancipation. It also shows a segmented education queue. On the one hand, it shows the white upper, middle and lower classes; the brown upper and middle classes; and the miniscule black upper class – all sharing the same educational institutions although all groups did not have equal access to all the institutions. On the other hand, Table 2.1 shows the white female lower-class, the brown lower-class, and the black middle and lower-classes all sharing another set of educational institutions.

The presentation of a segmented queue in education, following Emancipation, is similar to Smith's (1965) notion of the plural society and Curtin's (1975) notion of two Jamaicas. The queue is represented in two segments not only because two different sets of education institutions were shared by different groups in the society, but also because these two sets of institutions were administered separately. In essence, the different social groups were in control of the institutions educating their children. The queue reflected both the inequalities that obtained between groups in their access to educational opportunities and the social segregation that obtained in the Jamaican society at that time.

Table 2.1 shows that the top position in the education queue was held by males from the white upper class – mainly planters, planting attorneys and top colonial bureaucrats. Their elementary education was provided at home by paid private tutors, mainly governesses. Their secondary education was obtained from mainly English public schools like Charterhouse, Eton or Harrow. Some went on to university, mainly Cambridge and Oxford. Brathwaite (1971) reported that between 1770 and 1820, 229 Jamaicans went to Oxford and Cambridge, and of those, 33 sat in the Assembly at some time during the fifty-year period of his study. These 229 Jamaicans were all male and the majority were from the white upper-class.

Next in the queue were brown upper-class males – mainly planters and a few planting attorneys. Their education followed the same pattern as the Whites except that the proportion going to English public schools and universities was less. Next in line were the white middle-class males – mainly small settlers, penkeepers and professionals. Their children received their education in private day schools up to about age nine and then went on to trust schools mainly as paying students. A few of their sons went on to university.

Next in the queue were the white lower-class males, the brown middle-class males, and the black upper-class males. The white lower-class males were the target group for philanthropy in education in the slave society. Vestry and trust schools were established for them: boys of poor white families who could not afford to educate them. They attended schools as "foundationers" – beneficiaries of bequests or the benevolence of the church – and therefore received their education free of cost. Brown middle-class and black upper-class males shared the same educational provisions as these white lower-class males, but they had to pay the fees charged by the trust or parochial schools. It should be noted that the access of free coloureds, Browns and Blacks, to trust schools only occurred after 1815 (Brathwaite 1971), and that there was only a tiny number of Blacks who were upper class. The theological college offered the main route of further education for boys of these social groups.

The first girls in the education queue were daughters of the white middle-class and brown upper-class families. They received their education in private schools followed by education in the trust schools. A few went on to finishing school. They were followed by girls of the brown middle class and black upper class who did not benefit from finishing school exposure. It should be noted that these girls received more or less the same liberal education that was offered to boys. The only difference was that sewing was included in their curriculum.

The position of the white upper-class female is most interesting. She occupied the lowest position in the upper segment of the education queue. These white-upper class females were educated at home by governesses and then in finishing schools in Europe. The position of white upper-class girls in this segment of the queue reflects the fact that their position in society depended on race and class and the advantages these conferred in finding a husband on whom their future status would depend. The type and content of their education were geared to making them good mothers and wives of the masters and the mistresses of the greathouse. Their education, therefore was vocational and lacked the liberal elements received by white and brown upper and middle-class boys and white and brown middle-class girls. These latter were receiving education that was negotiable in the marketplace, while the upper-class girls were receiving education that fitted them only for their roles of wives and mothers in the greathouse.

When Segment A of the education queue is examined it should be noted that males occupied top positions and females the middle and lower positions. It would appear that in this segment of the queue gender took precedence over class in the interaction between race, class, and gender in forming the queue, thus ensuring the greater access of males of this segment to educational opportunities.

In Segment B of the queue the top positions were occupied by black middle-class and brown lower-class males, although they occupied the ninth position in the queue. Lower-class girls, of all racial groups, occupy the lowest position in the queue in this segment and overall.

Observations on the Education Queue

There are several observations that must be made concerning the education queue that obtained in the years immediately following Emancipation. These can be summarized briefly as follows:

1. The segmented nature of the education queue reflected the past organization of the society as slave and free. The Whites, most Browns and Jews and some Blacks were free, while most Blacks and some Browns were slaves. The segmentation of the queue reflected this history.
2. The white lower class occupied a niche in society that was not far removed from that of slaves. In terms of education, however, provisions were always made for boys of this group to have access to educational opportunities similar to those available to middle-class Whites and upper and middle-class brown males. Not so for lower-class white girls. Their position was at the bottom of the education queue alongside their lower-class brown and black sisters. In the main, white lower-class girls were kept out of school because the institutions to which they had access would bring them into contact with mainly black lower-class males. The point to note is that the advancement of white lower-class females did not depend upon education but on marriage to some successful white or brown male.

Table 2.2 The Differences between Expected and Actual Positions: Segment A

Segment A *Expected Education Queue*	**Segment A** *Actual Education Queue*
White upper-class boys	White upper-class boys
White middle-class boys	Brown upper-class boys
White lower-class boys	White middle-class boys
Brown upper-class boys	White lower-class boys
Brown middle-class boys	Brown middle-class boys
Brown lower-class boys	Brown upper-class girls
White upper-class girls	White middle-class girls
White middle-class girls	Brown middle-class girls
White lower-class girls	White upper-class girls
Brown upper-class girls	
Brown middle-class girls	
Brown lower-class girls	

Source: Latrobe Report (1837) Schedule B.

3. In each segment of the queue, males occupied the top positions and females the bottom positions, indicating that following emancipation the education queue was dominated by colour/status and gender. Combinations of colour and status determined the segmentation of the queue into two segments, but within each segment gender dominated: boys occupied the top positions and girls the lower positions. Even then, the positions in the queue were not entirely consistent with the expectations of the applied logic of the operational absolutes to the school system. This point can be illustrated in Table 2.2.

The differences between the education queue that is expected by simply applying the logic of the operational absolutes to the education system and the place queue actually observed are due to at least five principal factors.

1. Lower-class Whites and Browns, with the exception of lower-class white boys, occupied the same education niche as the groups composing Segment B of the queue. That is, historic social organizational factors in the society created an arbitrary break in the place structure that does not follow the strict logic of the place queue.
2. The actual education queue is a product not only of the application of the general place queue to the school system but also the interaction of the school system with other institutions and the rational actions suggested by those interactions. For example, the white upper class educated their sons and daughters in distinctly different ways. Their sons were given a sound liberal education while their daughters were given basic education and then exposed to finishing school. The brown upper class, by virtue of wealth and special privileges granted to particular families, had access to similar educational opportunities as the white upper class and sought the same type of education for their children. However, they sought to give their daughters a sound liberal education in addition to finishing school exposure.
3. The fact that the brown upper class sought a better education for their daughters than the white upper class seems related to the more secure social position of the latter, based on colour alone.
4. While boys hold the top positions in each segment of the education queue, when the queue is examined as a whole girls of the white and brown upper and middle class occupy higher positions than boys from the black middle class and brown and black lower class. In other words male hegemony is not uniform across the queue, it is segmented and interrupted by a female buffer based on colour and class.

5. The black lower-class female is the most marginalized group in the queue. While her brown and white sisters may entertain realistic hopes of social advancement through marriage to men of higher socioeconomic standing, she cannot realistically entertain such dreams. The black lower-class female's position in society immediately following Emancipation was not associated with any prospects of upward social mobility through education, occupation or marriage. Her position was almost without hope.

The Elementary School Teaching Occupation

It is necessary to locate the elementary school teaching occupation within the place structure given the segmentation that marked the place

Table 2.3 Private School Teachers by Gender 1837

Parish	Men		Women		Total
	N	%	N	%	
Kingston	21	21.4	77	78.6	98
Other parishes	15	57.7	11	42.3	26
Totals	36	29.0	88	71.0	124

Source: Latrobe Report (1837) Schedule B.

structure of the Jamaican society in the post-Emancipation period. Among the white and brown upper and middle-status groups elementary school teaching was not among the top rank of occupations to which members of this group aspired. However, it was a respectable occupation for members of the group to pursue.

Table 2.3 shows that the majority of the private school teachers in Kingston were female while in the other parishes the majority were male. In the island as a whole 29 per cent of private school teachers were men while 71 per cent were female. Latrobe reported that the majority of private school teachers in Kingston, male and female, were Jews. Approximately 80 per cent, 20 of the 21 male and 58 of the 77 female, of private school teachers were Jews. It seems reasonable to infer that in the years immediately after Emancipation private elementary school teaching in Jamaica was largely a brown middle-class female occupation. Latrobe reported that the teachers in the denominational elementary school system in 1837 fell into four categories:

1. European men recruited from Britain by the various missionary societies to schools in the newly created system.
2. White men and women, European or Creole, recruited locally.

3. Adult brown men and women born on thc island.
4. Young men and women who attended and recently left the normal and larger schools on the island.

The Latrobe Report shows that the majority of teachers in the denominational school system were male although the system employed a significant number of female teachers. In contrast to the private system which employed more women than men as teachers, the denominational system employed more men than women as teachers. The reason for this gender difference in the composition of teachers in the two systems related to the fact that through the Negro Education Grant the denominations recruited many white males to staff the newly created system of mass education.

Latrobe stated that brown men and women constituted 40 per cent of the teachers. Given the fact that most of the young men and women who would have attended normal and trust schools in Jamaica at that time would have been white or brown, it is not unreasonable to infer that at its inauguration the denominational elementary school teaching occupation was a white and brown middle-class male occupation.

The pay structure for teachers is worth noting. White married men were paid more than their single counterparts. Whites were paid more than Browns and men were paid more than women. The salary scale of the Church Missionary Society was as follows:

White married men	240 pounds sterling per annum
White single men	200 pounds sterling per annum
Brown men	70 to 140 pounds sterling per annum
Brown women	30 to 80 pounds sterling per annum

For the brown teachers the salary varied with locality and the cost of living. Hence the brown female teacher could earn as little as 12.5 per cent of the salary earned by the married white male teacher.

The point to note is that this denominational elementary school system established to serve the children of ex-slaves, mainly Blacks, was at this stage funded mainly by the Negro Education Grant provided by the imperial Parliament. Also, in 1837 the denominational school system was only in its fourth year of existence and was focused mainly on providing infants up to six years old with education. Blacks, who received little or no formal education during slavery, would have had virtually no opportunity to take up teaching positions, except in very few instances related to a few outstanding individuals.

PREDICTIONS BASED ON PLACE THEORY

Having previously outlined the general principles of place theory and now having derived the general place structure of the Jamaican society and the education queue that existed in the years immediately following Emancipation, it should be possible to predict the course of gender changes in the public elementary school teaching occupation and in the enrolment of teachers' colleges set up to supply locally trained teachers. The predictions will be in the form of the following hypotheses:

1. Given the segmentation in the education queue and the separate control of the dual system of education by the groups they serve, it can be expected that Blacks and their allies will attempt to make the denominational system a parallel and equal schooling to the private/trust system, while the white and brown upper and middle-status groups will seek to make the denominational school system subordinate and inferior to the private/trust school system.
2. Where Blacks gain and retain control over the denominational school system, upward social mobility opportunities will be biased in favour of males. That is, opportunities to advance from elementary schools to teachers' colleges will be biased in favour of black males served by the denominational system.
3. Where control of the denominational system falls into the hands of the ruling élite through the state machinery, upward social mobility through education will be shifted in favour of black females.
4. Attempts to integrate the society and the school systems would lead to further bias in favour of black females gaining access to educational opportunities leading to upward social mobility.

Since place in society is the product of relative relationships between people and groups on the dimensions of power, status, resources, belief, and culture, then it will be imperative to examine the political, economic, sociological, ideological, and anthropological factors related to gender changes in teachers' colleges and elementary school teaching in Jamaica over the past one hundred and fifty years in order to test these hypotheses. Because of limitations in the available time and resources for conducting the study it was only possible to explore the political, economic, and social dimensions.

3

The Jamaican Case Study

This chapter will examine the period 1836 to 1990 in Jamaica with respect to the changes in the gender composition of teachers' college students, the changes in the gender composition of elementary school teachers, and the factors related to these changes. By so doing data will be provided to test the validity of the hypotheses postulated in chapter 2.

THE GENDER OF TEACHERS' COLLEGE STUDENTS

In examining the gender composition of teachers' college students it will be necessary to discuss some aspects of the institutional provisions, recruitment of students, enrolment and performances of students from 1836 to 1990.

The Institutional Provision

After Emancipation, through the Negro Education Grant, £5,000 was provided for the training of teachers in Normal Schools–teachers' training colleges. Grants were given to the Lady Mico Charity and various denominations which started such colleges. The system of education established for the children of the ex-slaves was denominational. It followed the English thinking at that time, that popular education was essentially a religious matter. In addition, the nonconformist church and the British government had been allies in the Emancipation movement; hence, they accepted the obligation to create the infra-structural bases of a free society. The denominational system consisted of two elements – elementary schools and teacher training colleges.

Initially, the Lady Mico Charity and all the Protestant denominations, except the Methodists, started teachers' colleges. Children under six years of age were freed in 1834. They were available for full-time instruction. Schools and teacher training institutions during the Apprenticeship period concentrated on infants. In the scramble to staff the schools any suitable person was pressed into service. These included expatriate Whites, Browns and Blacks. Persons recruited to teach in the schools and to be trained in the Normal Schools included men and women. In 1832, the Moravians had, in fact, started a college at Refuge to train brown women as teachers. Several of these Normal Schools were indeed cottage-type operations with a master training a few students who lodged in his home. In 1845, government joined the foray in teacher training. Many Normal Schools, including that of the government and the Moravian college at Refuge, were short-lived. The Normal Schools which survived this initial burst of teacher training to become teacher training colleges were Mico, non-denominational; Calabar, Baptist; Fairfield, Moravian; and Montego Bay, Presbyterian.

Mico started in 1836 with twenty-one men and seven women admitted at irregular intervals during that year. From that coeducational beginning, it became a college which trained male teachers. Calabar, run by the Baptists, operated as a Normal School alongside its theological college. It trained male teachers. Fairfield, started by the Moravians in 1839, also trained male teachers, so did the Presbyterian College in Montego Bay. In other words, while in the first decade of the denominational system the institutional provision allowed for the training of male and female teachers, by 1850 all the colleges training teachers had become exclusively male institutions.

In 1861 the Moravians started a college, Bethlehem, to train female teachers for infant schools. Bethlehem, therefore became the only college offering teacher training to women. Even then, preparation at that college was for infant and not elementary schools.

Following the Morant Bay Rebellion, Governor John Peter Grant established a Government Training College for men in 1870. It was first located at Stony Hill and later relocated to Spanish Town. Its mission was to train teachers with competence in industrial and agricultural subjects.

The Commission mandated to inquire into the conditions of the juvenile population in 1879 included in its recommendations the establishment of a government college to train female teachers. Following strong representation through petitions from custodes, some clergy, and other influential persons, in 1885 government established a college to train female teachers – the Shortwood Teachers' Training College.

In 1877, the Presbyterians closed their college in Montego Bay. In 1890, the government closed its college for training male teachers. In 1899, the government withdrew all financial aid to denominational colleges training male teachers. This led to the closure of Fairfield in 1899 and Calabar in 1900.

St Joseph's Teachers' College was started in 1897 by the Roman Catholics. At the beginning of the twentieth century, therefore, the institutional provision for teacher training was as follows:

Mico	-	Male teachers
Bethlehem	-	Female teachers
St Joseph's	-	Female teachers
Shortwood	-	Female teachers

These institutional arrangements remained for fifty-five years until the opening of Moneague by the government in 1956. With Moneague, the concept of coeducation was reintroduced into teacher training. All new colleges have since been operated along these lines.

Additional colleges were added to the system following the opening of Moneague. These included West Indies College Teacher Training Division – a private college run by the Seventh Day Adventists; Church Teachers' College (1965) owned by the Anglican Church; Sam Sharpe Teachers' College established by government with World Bank assistance (1975); and Passley Gardens with United States Agency for International Development (USAID) assistance (1981).

Mico became coeducational in the late 1950s following the introduction of the new policy, while Bethlehem became coeducational in 1981. Shortwood has remained a college training female teachers only. St Joseph's has also remained a college training female teachers although for a short time it attempted coeducation.

Moneague was closed temporarily in 1985 but reopened in 1987. The institutional provision for training primary school teachers in Jamaica in 1990 was as shown below.

Bethlehem	-	Coeducational
Church	-	Coeducational
Mico	-	Coeducational
Passley Gardens	-	Coeducational
Sam Sharpe	-	Coeducational
Moneague	-	Coeducational
West Indies	-	Coeducational
St Joseph's	-	Female
Shortwood	-	Female

From the above it can be seen that currently there are no exclusively male teachers' colleges in Jamaica, while there are still two exclusively female colleges although the policy since the 1950s has been towards coeducation.

The institutional provision for the training of teachers from 1836 to 1990 could be classified into three distinct periods.

1. 1834 to 1899 – during which period institutions were single sex with a heavy bias toward the training of male teachers.
2. 1900 to 1955 – when institutions remained single sex but the bias was shifted to the training of female teachers.
3. 1956 to 1990 – during which period the policy of coeducation has predominated.

It should also be noted that since 1965 these colleges which before had trained elementary school teachers exclusively were diversified in terms of their mission and have been preparing teachers to work in secondary schools and special education. The only colleges that currently train primary school teachers exclusively are St Joseph's and Passley Gardens. Note must also be taken that Hamilton (1985) has shown that boys and girls in single sex schools perform better than boys and girls in coeducational institutions. However, there has been no review of the policy of coeducation in the post-Independence period.

Table 3.1 Teachers' College Enrolment 1870-1899

Year	Male		Female		Year	Male		Female	
	N	%	N	%		N	%	N	%
1870	79	88.8	10	11.2	1885	112	75.7	36	24.3
1871	93	93.0	7	7.0	1886	114	76.0	36	24.0
1872	98	92.5	8	7.5	1887	117	78.5	32	21.5
1873*	10	100.0	–	–	1888	119	77.3	35	22.7
1874	100	94.3	6	5.7	1889	No Report			
1875	89	93.7	6	6.3	1890	81	65.9	42	34.1
1876	89	92.7	7	7.3	1891	53	60.2	35	39.8
1877	90	92.8	7	7.2	1892	52	55.3	42	44.7
1878	94	91.3	9	8.7	1893	127	74.3	44	25.7
1879	81	90.0	9	10.0	1894	65	53.3	57	46.7
1880	75	90.4	8	9.6	1895	137	70.3	58	29.7
1881	75	90.4	8	9.6	1896	139	68.5	64	31.5
1882	86	91.5	8	8.5	1897	122	67.8	58	32.2
1883	88	91.7	8	8.3	1898	122	67.8	58	32.2
1884	90	91.8	8	8.2	1899	104	65.4	55	34.6

*Bethlehem, the only female college at that time, was closed for the year.
Source: Blue Books of Jamaica, 1870-1899.

Enrolment by Gender

It is convenient to examine the enrolment of teachers' colleges with respect to the gender of their students in the three periods specified above.

From Table 3.1, it can be seen that up to 1884, 90 per cent or more of the students enrolled in teachers' colleges were male. With the establishment of Shortwood in 1885, the proportion changed. On an average, two-thirds were male and one-third female up to 1899. In other words, not only was the institutional provision weighted in favour of male students but the enrolment also reflected that bias as well as the effort to change it.

Table 3.2 shows teachers' college enrolment in the years 1900 to 1909, 1930 to 1939, and 1949 to 1954.

Table 3.2 Teachers' College Enrolment, 1900-1955 (Selected Years)

Year	Male		Female	
	N	*%*	*N*	*%*
1900	76	58.0	55	42.0
1901	72	56.3	56	43.7
1902	72	55.4	58	44.6
1903	66	46.2	77	53.8
1904	72	49.0	75	51.0
1905	73	48.7	77	51.3
1906	68	47.6	75	52.4
1907	66	51.2	63	48.8
1908	68	47.6	75	52.4
1909	No Report*			
1930	56	41.5	79	58.5
1931	59	36.0	105	64.0
1932	50	31.8	107	68.2
1933	60	34.1	116	65.9
1934	57	34.3	109	65.7
1935	54	38.3	137	71.7
1936	52	38.3	132	71.7
1937	No Report			
1938	9	31.6	128	68.4
1939	No Report			
1949	92	32.4	192	67.6
1950	No Report			
1951	94	32.0	200	68.0
1952	105	34.4	200	65.0
1953	108	34.1	209	65.9
1954	109	32.1	231	67.9
1955	No Report			

* The reports from these years have not been located from any local source.
This table was compiled from statistics in the Blue Books and annual departmental reports for the years specified.

It can be seen from Table 3.2 that following the restructuring of the institutional provisions in 1899 in favour of females instead of males, by the first decade of the twentieth century, female students had achieved parity: by the 1930s, on an average, two-thirds of the students being trained as teachers were females and one-third was male. This position remained unchanged up to 1955. Clearly the restructuring of the institutional provision in 1899 shifted enrolment in favour of females, which was the intention.

Table 3.3 Teachers' College Enrolment 1958-1985 (Selected Years)

Year	Male		Female	
	N	%	N	%
1958	120	31.3	236	68.7
1963	244	25.1	729	74.9
1976-77*	704	16.9	3463	83.1
1977-78*	752	17.2	3616	82.8
1980-81*	604	17.2	2899	82.8
1984-85*	596	17.7	2771	82.3

* These figures represent the overall enrolment of the colleges. They exaggerate the percentage of male students enrolled in the primary teaching programme and underestimate the number of females.
The figures are compiled from Ministry of Education statistics for the years specified.

It can be seen from Table 3.3 that during the period of coeducation, the bias shifted even further in favour of female students. Table 3.4 shows that in 1984-85, 89.4 per cent of the students being prepared to teach in primary schools were females.

Table 3.3 shows that in 1958 the number of primary school teachers in training was 356. Table 3.4 shows that by 1984-85 the number in training had increased to 1056. At the same time the proportion of

Table 3.4 Students Enrolled in the Primary Programme in Teachers' Colleges 1984-85

College	Male		Female	
	N	%	N	%
Bethlehem	13	13.3	85	86.7
Church	–	–	–	–
Mico	21	22.1	74	77.9
Moneague	4	2.7	145	97.3
Passley Gardens	37	24.0	117	76.0
St Joseph's	–	–	298	100.0
Sam Sharpe	37	23.3	122	76.7
Shortwood	–	–	103	100.0
Total	112	10.6	944	89.4

Compiled from Ministry of Education statistics for 1984-85

female students had also increased from approximately 67 per cent to nearly 90 per cent.

The twin policies of dramatic expansion of teacher training and coeducation have actually worsened the situation of the number of male teachers being prepared for primary education. Put another way, the policy of single sex institution seems to have worked to preserve a better balance between the sexes in teachers' colleges than the current policy of coeducation. In moving to meet the target of a fully trained primary school teaching force in the post-Independence period, even fewer men have been recruited and trained as primary school teachers.

Teacher Recruitment and Supply

In completing the picture of the interrelationship between teachers' colleges and the gender structure of the teaching force in primary schools, it is necessary to look at the available information on the recruitment of students by the college from the school system and the supply of college trained teachers to the schools. From the outset, there seems to have been almost a reciprocal relationship between students recruited from the school system and the supply of teachers to the elementary schools from the teachers' colleges.

Teacher Recruitment

From the 1840s promising students from elementary schools were recruited as pupil teachers at age 14. They were given limited teaching duties, instructed in a set curriculum which prepared them for entry to college. They were also required to sit certain examinations, on the basis of which (performance and qualifications) they would gain entry to the teachers' college (Cundall 1914: 34-35). After being trained as teachers they would return to the elementary school. The relationship between elementary school and teachers' college in terms of recruitment and supply was direct, mediated only by the pupil-teacher system.

Between 1834 and 1899, it would appear that the majority of students recruited into the pupil-teacher system were male. Not all went to college to be trained. Many remained in the schools as unqualified teachers. Cundall commented on "the number of young men not technically prepared who were placed over schools prior to the time when the Education Department under Mr Capper allowed no one to be appointed as a teacher who had not been registered as qualified for the position" (Cundall 1914: 43).

Further evidence about recruitment for both employment in the schools and entry to teachers' colleges came from Superintendent

Inspector Capper, who was also a member of the Legislative Council. In a debate in the Council in 1891, Mr Capper stated that there was a difficulty in finding females who had met the minimum levels of education established for entry to teachers' colleges (*Proceedings, JLC* 1891-92: 17). Reference was made to the fact that not all of the available places had been filled at Shortwood and Bethlehem, the two colleges for females at that time.

After 1900, more females were employed as pupil-teachers and enrolled in colleges for training as teachers. It would appear that increased opportunities for women to enter teachers' colleges also resulted in increased employment opportunities both as pupil-teachers and as trained teachers.

The pupil-teacher system established the pattern of teachers' colleges recruiting the vast majority of their students from the elementary system. This persisted even after the pupil-teacher system was abolished. Persons eighteen years of age and over, who had passed the Jamaica Local Examinations, were recruited in elementary schools as untrained teachers. These untrained teachers became the major source of students recruited to teachers' colleges. Direct entry from secondary schools was the exception, rather than the rule, before the 1970s.

Since the late 1970s, the number of untrained teachers has declined steadily as the primary teaching force has increased its proportion of trained teachers. In 1984-85, approximately 90 per cent of primary school teachers were trained. The pattern that has emerged in the 1980s is that of recruits for teachers' colleges coming directly from secondary school leavers. The numbers coming from the ranks of untrained teachers have diminished as that group has decreased in the primary school system.

The entry qualifications have changed dramatically over the 150-year period. First, it was based on performance in pupil-teacher examinations set by the Department of Education on an individual and, later, a group basis (Cundall 1914: 43). Secondly, it was based on performance in the Jamaica Local Examinations set by the Department of Education. In the 1960s the Jamaica School Certificate (JSC) of the Ministry of Education replaced the Jamaica Local Examinations as the basis of entry. To enter the primary teacher training programme, candidates were required to have five passes in the JSC, including English and Mathematics. Since 1981, entry to the primary teacher programme is secured with four passes in the Caribbean Examination Council (CXC) General Proficiency level at Grade I or II, including English, and a pass in Mathematics at least at the level of Basic II.

The question is whether the higher entry requirements and different educational background of the students mean that students from different social backgrounds are being recruited to be trained as primary school teachers. Tables 3.5 and 3.6 show the geographical areas of Jamaica from which students of Bethlehem and St Joseph's were recruited in the years 1932, 1942, 1952, 1962, 1972, and 1982. Data on all students entering the two colleges in the years specified were obtained from the college records. Morrissey (1984) has developed a rural-urban stratification of Jamaica based on criteria which include the following definitions:

Stratum A	– Metropolitan centre	–	population in excess of 500,000
Stratum B	– Urban areas	–	population of 20,000 - 500,000
Stratum C	– Small town	–	population of 2,000 - 20,000
Stratum D	– Rural areas	–	settlements not meeting the minimum criteria for small towns and other localities with dispersed population

Morrissey reported that in 1982 the percentage of the Jamaican population living in the four strata were as follows: Kingston Metropolitan Area, 27.1; urban areas, 10.3; small towns, 11.3; and rural areas, 51.3. Using the home addresses of the students, they were placed in one of the rural-urban strata shown above. The results of this classification of these students are shown in Tables 3.5 and 3.6.

These Tables also show that students recruited for training as primary school teachers continued to come mainly from the same

Table 3.5 Urban-Rural Background of Students: Bethlehem Teachers' College 1932-1982

	Kingston*		Urban area**		Small town		Rural area	
	N	*%*	*N*	*%*	*N*	*%*	*N*	*%*
1932	2	10.5	–	–	3	15.8	14	73.7
1942	2	8.3	1	4.2	4	16.7	17	70.9
1952	4	12.5	–	–	3	9.4	25	78.1
1962	–	–	1	3.0	3	9.1	29	87.9
1972	4	5.0	2	2.5	12	14.8	63	77.8
1982***	–	–	1	2.9	8	22.7	26	74.3

* Metropolitan area
** MoBay, Mandeville, May Pen, Spanish Town
*** Both male and female for the year 1982

Data compiled from college records.

geographical strata – rural areas. While the students of 1972 and 1982 were better qualified and came from different educational backgrounds, they continued to come from the same geographical areas of Jamaica. They were mainly the sons and daughters of the black peasantry. While they took a different educational route and attained higher educational qualifications, they ended up at the same occupational destination: primary school teaching. The pattern is the same, despite the fact that St Joseph's is an urban college and Bethlehem a rural one.

Table 3.6 Urban-Rural Background of Students: St Joseph's Teachers' College 1942-1982

Years	Kingston*		Urban area**		Small town		Rural area		Unknown	
	N	%	N	%	N	%	N	%	N	%
1942	5	33.3	–	–	–	–	9	60.0	5	6.6
1952	2	10.0	–	–	2	10.0	15	75.0	1	5.0
1962	11	25.0	1	2.3	10	22.7	22	50.0	–	–
1972	27	26.0	6	5.8	15	14.4	54	51.9	2	1.9
1982***	19	25.6	11	12.5	14	15.9	44	50.0	–	–

* Metropolitan area
** MoBay, Mandeville, May Pen, Spanish Town
*** Both male and female for the year 1982

Data compiled from college records.

Teacher Supply

With respect to teacher supply, Cundall (1914) commented that "if the number of youths trained by Presbyterians, Moravians, Baptists and at the Spanish Town College could be given, their joint contribution to the advancement of the elementary schools of the island would have helped inquirers to understand how widespread the earnest endeavour has been to promote through this agency, the best interests of the people of Jamaica" (D'Oyley 1979: 31). He stated that the Normal Department of Calabar produced 235 male teachers between 1855 and 1900. He further stated that during the period 1836 to 1896, Mico had trained 694 students, and that of the 960 teachers in elementary schools in that year, about 400 had no college training. He concluded that of those that had been trained, a large proportion had come from Mico. D'oyley reported that between 1870 and 1884 the government college trained 75 male teachers. Up to 1900, the supply of teachers from the colleges was predominantly male (Morrissey 1984: 101-23).

It can be seen from Table 3.7 that after the establishment of Shortwood in 1885 about one-third of the students enrolled in colleges after this year were female, but this is not reflected in the pass rate for third year students during the period 1890 to 1901. A significantly larger proportion of men were remaining in college for three years and were obtaining the certification at the end of the course. By the 1930s, however, female students were remaining in college for the three years and were obtaining the certificate qualification, based on their third year performance, in numbers more or less in keeping with their proportion of the enrolment. This position obtained up to the late 1950s.

While the data for some years of the 1960s indicate that women were outperforming men, the data for more recent years suggest that male and female are graduating in proportion to their numbers in the college population. These data would suggest that it was some thirty years before women were able to make full use of the opportunities provided for them. But after this initial period, they have performed on par with their male counterparts and, at times, performed better.

The interesting point to note is the reversal that has taken place with respect to perception of male and female students in the intervening period. College personnel now complain of the difficulty in obtaining suitably qualified male students for entry to college. This is the exact opposite of the case put forward by Capper in 1891.

Table 3.7 Teachers' College Third Year Passes 1890-1985 (Selected Years)

Year	Male		Female		Year	Male		Female	
	N	%	N	%		N	%	N	%
1890	-	-	-	-	1946	28	36.4	49	63.6
1891	-	-	-	-	1950	32	33.3	64	66.7
1892	-	-	-	-	1957	46	39.0	72	61.0
1897	21	87.5	3	12.5					
1898	43	89.6	5	10.4	1960	33	12.2	237	87.8
1899	24	75.0	8	25.0	1961	44	13.8	276	86.2
1901	25	75.8	8	24.2	1962	57	17.4	271	82.6
					1963	72	21.0	271	79.0
1929	19	36.5	33	63.5	1964	55	18.3	246	81.7
1930	17	42.5	23	57.5					
1931	17	30.4	29	69.6	1976-7	98	20.7	375	79.3
1932	15	28.8	37	71.2	1977-8	88	13.8	550	86.2
1933	19	30.6	43	69.4	1980-1	109	17.5	514	82.5
1934	16	25.4	47	74.6	1984-5	36	13.0	240	87.0
1935	23	31.5	50	68.5					
1936	17	30.9	38	69.1					
1938	23	44.2	29	55.8					

Source: Departmental Reports and Ministry of Education statistics, 1890-1985.

It would appear that during the period 1834-1899, not only did the institutional provision and college enrolment favour males; so too did the recruitment, supply, and socialization patterns. It does not appear that women forced their way into being recruited for training in colleges by virtue of overwhelming numbers among the pupil-teachers, or through superior performance in the pupil-teacher examinations. Supply and demand factors did not appear to have contributed to the change in the institutional provision in favour of females in the period 1885 to 1900. Rather, increased institutional provision for females to be trained as teachers gradually created the circumstances for women to overcome the disadvantages they suffered from their historical exclusion from educational opportunities in the higher levels of the education system. However, having overcome these disadvantages, women have not only equalled but surpassed men in their performance in teacher education.

The available evidence seems to suggest that the decision to restructure the institutional provision in favour of female teachers made recruitment and training opportunities more available for women in the teaching profession. The period 1900 to 1955 appears to have been one during which more training and employment opportunities opened up for black women to become teachers. The period 1956 to the present has seen women becoming more entrenched as primary school teachers. The essence of the change over the 150-year period is that the black woman has replaced the black man as the mainstay of the primary school teaching force.

Foster (1982: 3) has observed that history frequently reminds us of the continuities rather than the discontinuities that characterize societies undergoing rapid social change. Even the most profound political revolutions leave untouched much more than they destroy, and this seems pertinent when we examine the educational policies pursued by post-colonial nations. Certainly, no policy in the postwar or post-Independence period has made any fundamental structural difference with respect to the institutional provision, enrolment, recruitment, and supply patterns and interrelationships of teachers' colleges with the teaching profession and school systems and their relationship with the society.

THE GENDER OF ELEMENTARY SCHOOL TEACHERS

Latrobe in his 1837 survey of education in Jamaica found 183 elementary schools with an enrolment of 12,580 pupils and an establishment of 257 teachers. Of these 257 teachers, 153 were men and 104 were women. Latrobe further reported that of the 257 teachers 102 (41 men and 61 women) were coloured and the rest were white. The vast majority of the white teachers, 112 men and 43 women, had been recruited from Britain by the various missionary societies. Very few creole Whites were employed in the denominational system. The term "free people of colour" had been used during slavery for Jews and free Mulattoes and Blacks. Latrobe's classification of 102 teachers as coloured has to be understood against this background.

Earlier in this chapter it was said that at the inauguration of the denominational system, elementary school teaching was largely staffed by expatriate white and local brown teachers. It was therefore mainly a white and brown occupation. Whites were paid more than Browns and men were paid more than women. Among Whites married men were paid more than single men. One consequence of this pay structure was that brown women earned one-eighth of the salary of white married men.

The composition of elementary school teaching and its paid structure was due mainly to the fact that the Negro Education Grant of 1834 to 1846 allowed the missionary societies to recruit teachers from Britain and pay them at much higher rates than those recruited locally. The termination of the grant in 1846 led to the abandonment of that recruiting policy and to drastic changes in the composition of the elementary school teaching force.

Table 3.8 Gender of Elementary School Teachers in Jamaica 1837-1990 (Selected Years)

	Male		**Female**	
Year	***N***	***%***	***N***	***%***
1837	153	59.5	104	40.5
1872	460	90.5	48	9.5
1899	815	78.4	225	21.6
1951	881	20.9	3341	79.1
1975	1558	15.1	8732	84.9
1985	1280	12.4	9040	87.6
1990	1165	11.6	8910	88.4

Source: Latrobe (1837) and Department and Ministry of Education Reports.

Table 3.8 shows that elementary school teaching at its inauguration had a majority of male teachers, but women constituted a significant minority, 40.5 per cent. By 1872 the proportion of men had risen to over 90 per cent. At the end of the nineteenth century men were still the vast majority among elementary school teachers. In the twentieth century, however, the proportion of men in elementary school teaching has declined steadily while women have become the vast majority. In 1990 women were 88.4 per cent of the primary school teachers while men constituted only 11.6 per cent of all primary school teachers. Figure 3.1 shows the transformation graphically and dramatically.

Before attempting to account for the gender changes among elementary school teachers it is necessary to discuss changes in the racial/colour composition of these teachers from the position described by Latrobe in 1837. The point has been made previously that the Negro Education Grant permitted missionary societies to recruit teachers from Britain thus accounting for the fact that Whites constituted the majority of elementary school teachers in the first decade of the denomination's existence.

Figure 3.1 Gender of Elementary School Teachers in Jamaica 1837-1990

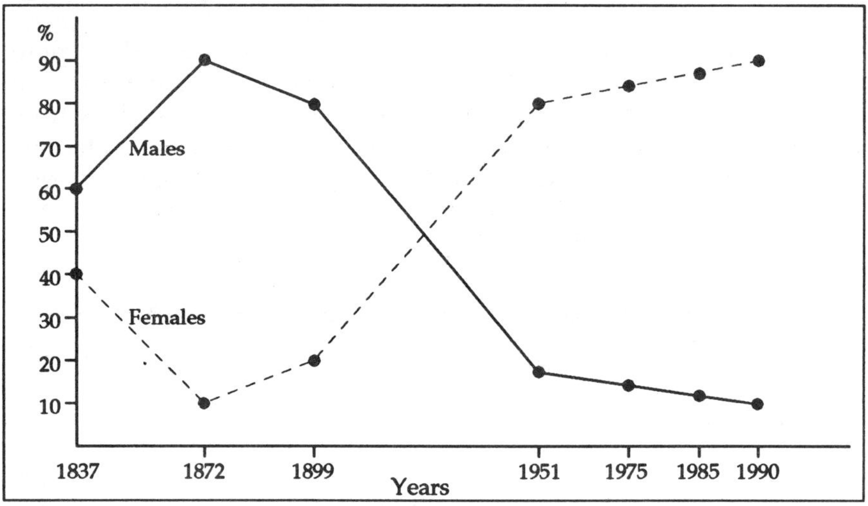

An important point to note is that all denominations did not benefit equally from the Negro Education Grant. The Anglican Church, the established church, was the major beneficiary. That denomination was therefore most seriously affected by the termination of the grant. The Anglican work in elementary education declined in both size and influence following the termination of the Negro Education Grant.

The reverse was true of the denominations that benefited least from imperial assistance. The size and influence of their work in elementary education increased. The Baptists did not accept imperial assistance, while the Moravians received very little. These two denominations had opted to recruit and train local teachers from the outset, hence their establishment of their own teacher training colleges, Calabar and Fairfield respectively. With the termination of the Negro Education Grant all denominations were virtually forced to follow the recruitment and training policies that had been adopted by the Baptists and the Moravians.

Given the strong connections of the Baptists and the Moravians with the ex-slave population it would be expected that recruitment of local teachers would result in the recruitment of Blacks. All the eyewitness reports of the period indicate that this was indeed the case. Two quotations should be sufficient to make the point.

Governor Henry Barkly (1854) commenting on the state of elementary education in 1853 stated that the general standard of teachers was not very high "owing to the want of qualified masters, but efforts are being made by the Mico Trustees, at the training institution in Kingston, by the Baptists at Calabar College, and by the Presbyterians at their academy of Montego Bay to rectify this defect, and I have met with very intelligent native teachers trained at one or other of these establishments." The term *native* was the diplomatic one often used at that time to refer to the ex-slaves and their descendants.

Retired Inspector Plummer, addressing the Social Science Congress in Manchester, England in 1866, was not as complimentary as the governor in describing the native teachers recruited locally to staff the elementary schools. The retired Inspector (Plummer 1866) stated:

> This inadequate pay can only command the services of the most inefficient and ignorant set of men in the educational field, and instruction exists only in name. If you visit one of the country schools you would find the poor teacher an ignorant uneducated man not decently clad, with his ragged dirty pupils around him, with probably one book among them, and in a great many instances, without any book at all, unprovided with either desks or benches.

Plummer was attempting to explain to the Social Science Congress the underlying causes for the Morant Bay Rebellion. He was highlighting the hostile, discriminatory, and parsimonious policies and practices of the planter-controlled Assembly with respect to elementary education, and his own frustration of submitting numerous reports and recommendations that were only tabled in the Assembly but never acted upon. In making his point, Plummer's description of the "native teachers and pupils" was negative and demeaning, to say the least.

Barkly's and Plummer's portrayals of the black teachers who replaced the expatriates following the termination of the Negro

Education Grant, have become stereotypes of elementary school teachers in Jamaica. Both agreed that these black teachers were sub-standard. One saw hope through the natural intelligence of the persons involved and opportunities for training; the other was disillusioned by virtue of the low salaries that the governing élite insisted on paying these teachers.

FACTORS RELATED TO THE GENDER CHANGES

A popular argument is that teaching is a low status and low paying profession to which men are not attracted and, even when they enter the profession, they do not remain in it. The data reported here do not support that position in so far as the attraction of men to and their retention in primary school teaching is concerned. Men do not appear to be leaving the teaching profession at any greater rate than women. Teachers' college enrolment, graduation rate, teacher supply, and the primary school teaching force all show between 85 per cent to 90 per cent of the primary school teaching force is trained; hence, there is a direct link between the gender structure of the teacher training institutions and the gender structure of the primary school teaching force. The low status and pay of teachers seem to be more the effect than the cause of not attracting male teachers.

The records suggest that the number of men being trained as primary school teachers is not simply a matter of the number of men offering themselves to be trained. At one stage, 90 per cent or more of the teachers in elementary schools were male. Between 1880 and 1900 deliberate attempts were made and decisions taken to alter the institutional structure in favour of female teachers. Colleges training male teachers were closed and colleges training female teachers were opened. The phenomenon being examined is the result of the institutional arrangements for teacher training and not individual interest. The pattern of teacher training in the twentieth century was actually set by decisions taken in the 1890s, in general, and 1899 in particular, when Fairfield and Calabar were closed.

The statistical data and historical evidence suggest a causal relationship between the institutional arrangements for teacher training and the recruitment, enrolment, supply, and employment of primary school teachers. Changes in the institutional arrangements have caused changes in teacher recruitment, enrolment, supply, and employment patterns. One can speak, meaningfully, of an institutional cause and the recruitment, enrolment, supply, and employment effects in primary school teacher training over the past 150 years in Jamaica. When the institutional arrangements favoured men in the nineteenth century, so did recruitment, enrolment, supply, and employment patterns. Changes in the institutional provision to favour female students resulted in corresponding changes in recruitment, enrolment, supply, and employment patterns in the first half of the twentieth century. For the fifty-six years that the institutional arrangements remained constant, so also did recruitment, enrolment, supply, and employment patterns. Further changes to the institutional arrangements in 1956 brought corresponding changes in these patterns thereafter.

The implications of this relationship are that a careful study of the factors which have shaped and changed the institutional arrangements over the past 150 years should reveal the crucial factors determining recruitment, enrolment, supply and employment patterns in teachers' colleges and primary schools. The record points to three critical periods in the history of teachers' colleges.

(a) The period between 1834 to 1865 when teacher education became institutionalized;
(b) the period 1885 to 1900 when the change was made to shift the bias away from training male teachers towards training female teachers; and
(c) the period after 1956 when teachers' colleges were dramatically expanded and coeducation introduced.

In the discussion which follows some attention will be given to the sociological, economic, and political forces operative in all three periods as these relate to the shaping of teacher training and primary school teaching. Particular attention, however, will be given to the period 1885 to 1900 since this is the most definitive period relative to the focus of this study.

FORCES SHAPING TEACHER TRAINING

Sociological Factors

Curtin (1955: 42-43) described the society emerging after Emancipation as two Jamaicas divided along ethnic lines: Anglo-Jamaica comprising two classes, Whites on the one hand and Browns and Jews on the other; and Afro-Jamaica consisting of Blacks. Apart from the law and legal institutions, they shared little else. The society, then, could properly be described as plural, where one accepts Smith's definition of pluralism (Smith 1965). Smith defined pluralism as the "condition in which members of a common society are internally distinguished by fundamental differences in the institutional practice ... such differences ... normally cluster, and by their cluster they simultaneously identify institutionally distinct aggregates or groups, and establish deep social divisions between them".

The institutional structure of the education system in the post-Emancipation period, 1834 to 1865, reflected the pluralism of the society. Only elementary education was offered in the colony. All parents paid fees for their children. However, education was offered along ethnic lines through the endowed and denominational systems. The Browns, Jews and poorer Whites attended the endowed schools; the Blacks and poorer Browns the denominational schools. The social cleavages between these racial groups were reflected in the institutional arrangements for schooling. The endowed and denominational schools were organized as parallel systems delivering the same type of education to different ethnic groups.

Link Between Blacks and Teachers' Colleges

The link between teachers' colleges and black males in the post-Emancipation period is a sociological fact which has not yet been fully explained. As was pointed out previously, initially mostly Whites and Browns, males and females, were recruited as primary school teachers and for teacher training. The pattern that emerged from this beginning, however, was that of black males constituting the vast majority of both teachers and recruits for training. Miller accounts for the linkage between Blacks and elementary school teachers in terms of the movement of some ex-slaves away from the plantation to seek a new life. The essence of his explanation is outlined as follows:

1. The Jamaican peasantry arose following Emancipation when some ex-slaves left the plantations and established free villages. The act of leaving the plantation was a manifestation of the resistance that had existed toward slavery and plantation life. It was a bold statement against white planter domination and an expression of black independence. Consequently, planters did everything to discourage and undermine the free villages. The Jamaican peasantry was therefore founded in the context of conflict between dominant and subordinate groups in the Jamaican society.
2. The free villages were built around the institutions of the family, the school, the church, and the small farm. Each of these four elements which constituted the infrastructure of these communities represented a significant departure from plantation life and slavery. Some comment is necessary about each of these four elements (Miller 1991: 174-75).

During slavery there was no room for the family as a parent-child group living in a home. There was still less room for the development of stable relationships among a wider circle of kin living in permanent contact and visiting one another regularly and freely. The residential unit in the plantation system was formed by the mother and children. The responsibility of maintaining and protecting it rested with the slave owner and not the father. Accordingly the father's place in the family was never secure. He had no externally sanctioned authority over the family or household and could be physically removed from it at any time.

The family living in a home close to other homes and with other families restored what slavery and plantation organization had broken. Fathers living permanently with their wives and children, and protecting their families were affirming and reestablishing what plantation organization and slavery had negated. The restoration of traditional family life, as it had been known and practised in Africa, was indicting and abandoning the matrifocal forms that slavery and plantation organization had fostered.

Education was considered by the planters to be subversive to both slavery and the plantation system. The most enlightened slaveowners had allowed some missionaries to teach the rudiments of reading to a few slaves, but this was as far as education went. It is not unfair to say that schooling for slaves and their children was nonexistent during slavery. Those who learned to read and count had done so largely on their own initiative and through self-instruction (Miller 1991: 175-77).

The establishment of schools for the children of former slaves, coupled with the opportunities for the most successful students to become teachers, represented a qualitative difference from what existed during slavery. The inauguration of schooling further represented the intention to break with the past. The school was the symbol of hope and the means of achieving a different future than that promised by agricultural labour on the plantation.

From several perspectives the small farm was probably the greatest symbol of freedom. It provided an alternative livelihood to the plantation. It made the owner independent of the planter. It transformed the ex-slave into an owner, instead of being owned. Farms of a certain size qualified the farmers to vote. This made them citizens. For all of these reasons the small holding was freedom itself. Miller (1991: 176) has other comments on this:

1. The church was the trade union, the political party, the citizen's association, and the commodity organization. The church was the very centre of community life and of socioeconomic survival. In

addition, it provided spiritual sustenance and moral guidance. In the free village, the church could operate in ways that would never have been tolerated on the plantation. Through the church, these black peasants had some influence and control over the denomination school system. They therefore had it within their power to participate in the school system largely on their terms.

2. In the family, the school, the church, and on the farm, patriarchal authority and patterns were reestablished with full theological backing. Marriage was reestablished as the norm for family life. Husbands/fathers were breadwinners and mothers were housewives caring for husbands and children. Men operated in the public sphere at the same time that women were returned to the private sphere. Teachers were men. So too were the leaders of the church. While the farm required the assistance of all members of the family, the fathers were in charge. Slavery had undermined patriarchy. The free villagers proposed to restore it.

In addition to the points made by Miller (1991), it should be noted that the British tradition to that point – and, certainly, in the Victorian era – was decidedly patriarchal. Most of the West African tribes that came to Jamaica – Ibo, Dahomenian, Yoruba and Congo – were patrilineal and patriarchal. Although the Akan tribes were matrilineal, men were still dominant. The man exercised his authority over his sisters' children and not his children, since the legacy of his family was passed down through her children and not his. Notwithstanding the influences of creolization and slavery, the Blacks after Emancipation, particularly those that established free villages, sought opportunities for the advancement of their sons more than they did for their daughters, in keeping with their African ancestry.

For whatever reason, the linkage between the black rural hill communities and teachers' colleges – and later theological colleges for those denominations that sought to train a black clergy – instituted a route of upward social mobility for Blacks. While some young men entered the theological college directly, others trained as teachers first and then, on the basis of their teaching qualification, pursued theological training.

Within the first fifty years – by 1884 – outstanding graduates had emerged from teachers' colleges. These included Rev. W.M. Webb, a Mico graduate turned Baptist Minister, who founded Westwood High School for Girls in Trelawny, and Robert Lindsay who became a tutor of the staff of Mico. With respect to Lindsay, Cundall (1914: 46) states "when appointed as tutor, some thought that his race was put on its trial, as they did not believe that black men would obey a black man; but they were mistaken".

Cundall (1914: 88-97) lists all past students of Mico living and working in Jamaica in 1913 by year of graduation, occupation, and the parish in which they worked. Of the 363 Miconians listed, approximately 95 per cent were in teaching, mainly in rural schools. The 18 who were not teaching included the following:

Minister of religion	-	9
Agricultural instructor	-	3
Probation service	-	1
Jamaica Railway employee	-	1
Journalist	-	1
Inspector of schools	-	1
Dentist	-	1
Barrister at law	-	1

While the number of Miconians at that time working outside of teaching was most modest – (a mere 5 per cent) – several had moved into occupations not previously pursued by Blacks in Jamaica. Teaching itself was a middle-class occupation and through the teachers' colleges, the route was established to other middle-class occupations.

Goulbourne in his work on the formation of the Jamaican Union of Teachers observed that "elementary school teaching became one of the main – if not the main – means of upward social mobility for the ambitious sons of the peasantry who saw no prospects of a satisfactory future on the land and who had no way of attending secondary school which held out the possibility of going to university or into civil service" (Goulbourne 1988: 105). Goulbourne went on to point out that in 1891, elementary school teachers formed the largest single occupational group of those categorized as "professional" workers in the colony. This was explained by the fact that education was the largest social service in the colony at that time. Eisner (1961: 166) commented on the rise of the number of "professional" workers in the colony between 1881 and 1921 and attributed it to the rapid growth of the number of teachers and civil servants over the period.

Teachers' College Graduates Blocked from the Civil Service

It should be noted that elementary school teachers were virtually blocked from entering the civil service. While discrimination against them may have been implicit and covert, in 1893, when civil service examinations were established as the means of entry to the Service, that discrimination became explicit and overt. The rules for determining how young men could obtain Civil Service appointments (Jamaica, Civil Service Examinations 1894) were as follows:

1. Competitive Examinations of Candidates for Third Class Clerkships in Jamaica will be held from time to time at such places in Jamaica as may be deemed expedient.
2. These examinations are open to all natural born subjects of Her Majesty, being of the prescribed age and good health and character. Provided nevertheless that persons who have been educated at a College for training teachers in Jamaica, aided from Public Funds, will not be eligible as candidates for competition for or nomination to public appointments till they have repaid the full amount expended from such Public Funds for their training. The amount is fixed on the basis of 35 pounds for each year during which the candidate has been under training, so that a candidate who has received three years training will have to repay, under the operation of this clause, the amount of 105 pounds. Such amount will be refunded in case of failure of the candidate to obtain an appointment.
3. A fee of five shillings will be required from every candidate attending a Preliminary Examination, and a further fee of one pound from every candidate admitted to the Competitive Examinations.

To be able to sit the civil service examinations in 1893, a graduate of a teachers' college would have to pay the full cost of his training (£105) in addition to the examinations fees. Given the fact that this amount would be more than three years' salary for most teachers, this clause excluded them from competing for posts in the civil service. By virtue of their education, teachers' college graduates could surely successfully compete for civil service posts. They had therefore to be excluded on other grounds.

What is as interesting is that the Jamaica Schools Commission, which had responsibility for preparatory and secondary schools, was given the responsibility to conduct the annual civil service examinations. Both the organizational arrangements and the examinations regulations clearly indicated the social linkages that were being established between the school system and the civil service. The virtual exclusion of Blacks from the civil service made teaching as an occupation even more important in their aspirations.

Competing Intentions in Education

From the beginning of the free society in 1834, there were two distinctly different social philosophies concerning how the society ought to be structured. For easy reference, one will be called the planter's view and the other the ex-slave's view. The planter's view was that the society ought to be structured along colour/class lines comprising a white upper class, a brown middle class, and a black working class (Campbell 1967, 1970). The Blacks would be wage labourers on the plantation or, at best, tradesmen. Accordingly, education for that class should socialize them to accept their place at the bottom of the social ladder, and provide literacy, agricultural, and industrial skills to prepare them for their specific vocational tasks.

The ex-slave's view was that of an open egalitarian non-racial society which permitted upward social mobility based upon ability, interest, and effort. Accordingly, a black person through education should rise socially in the society to any position. The curriculum of the school, therefore, needed to provide those subjects that would permit their socioeconomic progress. The Baptists certainly championed this social philosophy (Phillippo 1843: 198, 212).

By articulating and championing the social philosophy of the ex-slaves, the Baptists had a disproportionate influence on the curriculum of the denominational system as a whole. Each denomination had control over what was offered in its schools. However, because schooling was an important means of gaining and retaining members, if one denomination catered to views held by the Blacks and the others did not, then there was the likelihood of that denomination making membership gains at the expense of the others.

From the outset, the Assembly sought to promote agricultural and industrial education in elementary schools and teachers' colleges in keeping with the planter's philosophy. These efforts, including the establishment of industrial schools, seemed to have been foiled because of Baptist opposition, based on the argument that such education was intended to keep the black people in occupations not far removed from those engaged in during slavery (D'Oyley 1979: 13).

The differences in social philosophy as they applied to education, especially the curriculum, led to an almost perennial struggle between academic on the one hand, and agricultural and technical education on the other. In the 1850s, the curriculum in the teacher training division at Calabar included school management, the three R's, music, elocution, geography and geometry with a few of the students permitted to take courses in rhetoric, church history and Latin. In the Presbyterian institution, in addition to the normal subjects, the men were instructed in history, geography, mathematics, chemistry, Latin and theology. The government college set up to train male teachers in 1870 had a specific mandate to produce teachers of industrial education. D'Oyley points out that by 1877 when the college was relocated to Spanish Town, the whole emphasis had clearly shifted from the industrial to the academic. D'Oyley (1979: 21) observed: "Their curriculum was the customary one found in many denominational centres in the island at that time. Music was stressed. Industrial pursuits were considered essential, and the government required that staff members have industrial experience. Nevertheless, the industrial aspect of the school never succeeded".

For as long as the denominations retained control of the curriculum in their colleges, the government could not succeed with an industrial curriculum even in its own college.

By the end of the 1870s, shifts began to be made to adjust the institutional provision for education in favour of the colour/class philosophy. This was done in two stages. The first stage started in 1879 when the government began the process of taking over the endowments of the endowed schools and of reorganizing the institutions through the Jamaica Schools Commission into high schools, linked to Cambridge University external examinations. By so doing, the endowed schools were being adjusted to have a comparable structure to that which had evolved in the denominational system. Endowed elementary schools then led to high schooling in a similar fashion to the way in which denominational elementary schools led to teacher training colleges. The two systems were more or less similar at the time.

After researching the work of the Jamaica Schools Commission between 1879 and 1911, King came to the conclusion that "secondary schools developed in Jamaica in the first quarter of the nineteenth century, because the decision and policy makers felt that the middle classes deserved and needed an education superior to that being offered to the poorer classes in the elementary schools, and because the majority of the white ruling class could no longer afford to send their children home to England to be educated" (King 1972: 63). The curriculum in these schools was upgraded to include Latin, Greek, mathematics, natural sciences and modern languages. From as early as 1882, the reorganized endowed schools began to require their students to sit examinations offered by Cambridge University.

The second stage began when the government took over the denominational system in 1892: it was now in a position to adjust structurally the total educational system of the colony according to the colour-class social philosophy. This it did during the economic crisis of the late 1890s following the report of the Lumb Commission (1898). Before looking at how the systems were adjusted following the Lumb Commission, it is necessary to record the prevailing views of the ruling class about the education of Blacks, and boys in particular.

***

In the Legislative Council debate on industrial schools in 1893, Palache of Manchester (*Proceedings, JLC* 1893-94:86) adequately represented the views of his colleagues when he stated that "the class of education the people were receiving was not doing the country any material good ... the useful class of community were dying out and were being replaced with a half educated, vagrant class, men who as soon as they could read and write and thus got a little education, began to regard the most important class of labour in the county – agriculture and artisanship – with contempt and thought they must go into the civil service, or the stores and shops ..." Palache concluded that children should be made to see "that their own advancement and progress existed in devoting themselves to tilling the soil that enabled their fathers to build and get together the houses they had".

Andrew of Kingston and St Andrew supporting Palache said that the best system of education he knew at present was that which he saw at Alpha Cottage. He is recorded as having said: "... There the system was admirable. There were about 150 children who, besides being taught to read, write and count, were being taught the principles of agriculture, to become domestic servants and all the similar branches of knowledge with respect to technical education" (*Proceedings, JLC* 1893-94: 92).

The attitude of the elected members of the legislature in the 1890s to the education of black boys is best portrayed by the comments of Farquharson of St Elizabeth in the debate on the proposed establishment of the secondary school for boys, Cornwall College in Montego Bay. The JLC Proceedings report him as stating that "if they wanted scholars of another class let them be agricultural and industrial where the children could be taught agriculture and trades, and where they could make a living for themselves after they have left the school". If they had secondary education the boys would look upon trade and agriculture with contempt. Very few would obtain jobs in the higher positions hence they would become idle and vicious. "Let them receive such an education as will benefit their station in life" (*Proceedings, JLC* 1893-94: 93).

The recommendations accepted and implemented out of the Lumb Commission included the closure of the University College attached to the Jamaica High School, and the downgrading of the curriculum of elementary schools and teachers' colleges.

The subjects removed from the teachers' college curriculum were science, Latin, French, algebra, geometry, mechanics, trigonometry, elocution and instrumental music. The subjects in which the amount of instruction was reduced were geography, history, grammar, composition, and drawing. The subjects introduced were object lessons, laundry work, cooking, and manual instructions. Those in which the amount of instruction was extended were reading, school management, drill, agricultural instruction, and domestic economy (Gordon 1968: 128).

The changes in the curriculum of the teachers' colleges were consistent with changes made to the curriculum of the elementary schools where instruction in arithmetic, history, geography, grammar, composition, sewing, and drawing was reduced; reading, writing, dictation, agriculture, and drill were increased, and object lessons and manual instruction were introduced. Other subjects were eliminated (Gordon 1968: 124).

***

The structure of the system after this adjustment retained the essential cleavage between racial groups in the society. In the main, Blacks would attend downgraded elementary schools and teacher training colleges. Browns, Jews and Whites would attend preparatory schools and upgraded high schools. But no higher education would be available locally. Wealthy Whites and Browns would continue to send their children abroad for such education.

It is interesting to note that the University College was closed precisely at the time that its major problem was being solved – that of being able to recruit a sufficient number of suitably qualified students. It would appear that this adjustment may have been intended to put limits on the social mobility of Browns and Jews through education. Increasingly, top positions in the government service were being filled by expatriate Whites. This reversed the trend that had emerged in the post-Emancipation period for creole Whites and Browns to hold such positions.

It is also important to note that in these structural changes of the last decade of the nineteenth century, the social distinction between educational institutions was shifted from ethnic differentials to economic considerations. Elementary schools were now free. Preparatory schools were fee paying; high schools were also fee paying, but six scholarships were provided that were open to all children. Latin was a subject in the scholarship examinations; hence, only children already in high schools won the scholarships. High schools prepared students for university but only those children whose parents could afford to send them abroad could obtain that level of tertiary education. These reforms were all consistent with a social philosophy which sought to entrench the colour/class system of stratification through the institutional provisions in the educational system.

stratification through the institutional provisions in the educational system.

The reforms of 1892, taken together with the adjustments made following the implementation of some aspects of the recommendations of the Lumb Commission, meant that the former endowed system was now elevated to a superior position, while its counterpart the former denominational system was downgraded to an inferior status. The high school now offered a liberal education, complete with mathematics, the sciences, modern languages, the classics, literature and fine arts. The teachers' college on the other hand, was offering agriculture and manual instruction as its main emphases, in addition to literacy.

The ethnic distinctions between the two systems were being obscured by the financial differentials arising from class that were being introduced. The former endowed system remained fee paying while the former denominational – now state – system, was free. But class was only a very thin veneer superficially covering the deep racial difference that had existed between these types of schools throughout the nineteenth century. The fact that a scholarship system would permit a few children from the black elementary schools to enter the white and brown high schools did not change, fundamentally, the ethnic distinctions that had developed.

The educational reforms of the 1890s had the sociological consequences of supporting a system that would keep black people, male and female, at the bottom of the social ladder and marginal in social status. In this regard, the curriculum was used as the major instrument in the service of the planters' social philosophy. There is no evidence that sociological factors led directly to a preference for black female teachers as against black male teachers.

The social philosophy and its manifestations through the reform of the curriculum of the elementary school and teachers' college in 1899, following Lumb, as well as the impact of the reordering of the relationships between educational institutions had equally negative influences on both black men and women. Blacks, as a whole, were being consigned to and confirmed in an inferior social status and to menial occupations.

There is no evidence that the preference of the ruling class for black women, evident during slavery, survived into the free society and was translated into preference in teacher training for female teachers. The preference for black females was recreated in the free society. While sociological factors may have contributed indirectly to that recreation, they did not represent the "sufficient condition". Other factors were more directly involved.

Economic Factors

In examining the economic factors related to the decision to cut off all aid to denominational colleges which trained men, it is necessary to look at the general economy of the colony, especially in the 1890s, and the economics of the denominational educational system which effectively ended in 1900. It is virtually impossible to chronicle these two aspects separately. They are best understood in interrelationships during the periods 1834 to 1865, and 1865 to 1900 – that is post-Emancipation and post Morant Bay Rebellion.

Emancipation occurred during a period of general decline of the sugar economy. The decline worsened after the introduction of the Equalization of the Sugar Duties Act in 1846 which resulted in the loss of preferential treatment for West Indian sugar on the British market. During the period 1834 to 1845, the Jamaican Assembly made no financial contribution to the education of the ex-slaves or their children. The denominational educational system was established by external funds given by the British government through the Negro Education Grant and the voluntary contributions of missionary societies. Much of this money was raised in England. The British government contributed two-thirds of the cost of the school buildings and the missionary societies, one-third. While some local churches provided land (and the Blacks labour) for the erection of the schools, it is fair to say that the denominational system was capitalized mainly from external funds. The British government provided £30,000 annually from 1835 to 1842, after which the grant was reduced and phased out finally in 1845 (Eisner 1961: 328).

An additional amount of £5000 was provided for the establishment of Normal Schools. The Lady Mico Charity shared these grants with the denominations, but its schools were nondenominational. During the period up to 1845, the grant from the British government was used both for capital and recurrent expenditure.

The termination of external support for the denominational system coincided with worsening economic conditions in Jamaica. From 1845 the Assembly contributed £3000 per year for the denominational system, but this went to the establishment of the Department of Education which offered some quality control services through annual inspection of the schools. Local government support for education through the vestries went almost exclusively to the Anglican schools (Campbell 1970: 12-17).

The burden of financing the denominational system fell to the black parents who paid fees for the education of their children. At the same time that sugar and the plantations were in deep financial trouble leading to many closures, the parallel economy of the small free-holders producing staples for the domestic market was growing. From the 1840s small settlers began to market their surplus production on estates and in towns (some estates survived and remained profitable). While there was brief recovery of sugar prices from 1855 to 1860, the general picture of the economy was one of decline for the period 1834 to 1865, despite pockets of growth among small free-holders and some Kingston merchants.

Clearly, the recurrent resources of the denominations and of the parents could not fully sustain the size of the system that had been established with external assistance, given the economic conditions that prevailed and the lack of meaningful assistance from the state (Campbell 1970: 28-30). By the 1860s, denominational education was more or less at a standstill and a source of discontent.

Sir John Peter Grant who became governor after the Morant Bay Rebellion disestablished the Anglican Church and used the savings of approximately £30,000 annually to support the denominational system (Eisner 1961: 364; Black 1958: 207). The support was given in the following areas:

(a) grants to erect new school buildings based on the old two-thirds/one-third formula;
(b) a salary subsidy to teachers through the payment by result system, based on the Inspector's annual report. This subsidy was in addition to the amount received by each teacher from the fees collected;
(c) grants to support the enlargement of teachers' colleges and the training of additional teachers;
(d) an enlarged inspectorate;
(e) a new government college to train male teachers; and
(f) a university college to offer higher education.

State support for denominational education brought a new burst of activity from the denominations which received help from external sources to meet their one-third contribution. They engaged in a new round of school building. This time, the source of capital was more internal than external.

The 1871 census recorded 123,834 children of school age – five to fourteen years. By 1891 that population had grown by 33 per cent to 164,152. In 1871 there were 35,916 enrolled in the denominational system, while in 1891 the denominational system had 84,165 children enrolled, an increase of over 130 per cent (*Blue Books* 1871, 1891; *Reports, Education Department* 1871, 1891).

Table 3.9 Jamaican Population, 1871 and 1891

	Year	
	1871	**1891**
Total population	**506,154**	**639,491**
Blacks	392,707	487,771
Coloured	100,346	121,955
Whites	13,101	15,605
Indian	–	10,116
Chinese	–	481
Other	–	3,623
4-14-year-olds	123,834	164,152
Elementary enrolment	35,916	84,165

Source: Census figures for 1871 and 1891.

In the twenty-year period, not only had there been a high rate of natural increase of the school age population, but there had been an even greater increase in the social demand for and participation in education from the black population as evidenced by the phenomenal growth in enrolment over the period. A number of observations are necessary at this point.

Blacks constituted 77.6 per cent of the total population in 1871, and 76.3 per cent in 1891. Assuming that the school age population reflected the same racial structure as the total population, there would have been approximately 96,095 and 125,248 black children aged five to fourteen years in 1871 and 1891 respectively. Bearing in mind that some coloured children attended the denominational schools but only a few black children attended the endowed schools, it seems safe to infer that less than 30 per cent of the black children were enrolled in schools in 1871. On the other hand, by 1891, certainly, more than 55 per cent were enrolled (although the figure could be as high as 60 per cent). This is despite the fact that the school age population had increased by 33 per cent in the twenty-year period.

Even more impressive was the number of schools built by the denominations during the period 1868 to 1894. From Table 3.10 it can be seen that between 1868 and 1892 when the government took over the denominational system, the denominations had built 544 schools. Between 1868 and 1892 the number of schools had increased by 340 per cent.

Crown colony government through Governor John Peter Grant had promised to address the poor quality of education. The governor's promise was backed by financial measures and reforms. The machinery

Table 3.10 Number of Elementary Schools 1868-1900

Year	No. of schools	Year	No. of schools
1868	286	1891-92	888
1869	262	1892-93	912
1870	329	1893-94	957
1871	408	1894-95	962
1872	438	1895-96	932
1873	456	1896-97	924
1874	500	1897-98	913
1875	526	1898-99	893
1876	569	1899-1900	776
1877	583		
1878	617		
1879	646		

Source: Blue Books of Jamaica, 1868 to 1900

of the state was to promote social justice for Blacks and improve social services. More efficient primary education was promised and was being delivered.

The combination of favourable economic circumstances and state support brought increased participation in education by Blacks. The denominations responded positively by building over five hundred additional schools. However, this capital expansion of the denominational system stretched the recurrent resources of the denominations to the limit or even beyond.

Enrolment in teachers' colleges increased from 89 in 1870 to 154 by 1889 (*Reports, Education Department* 1870, 1889), and the number of trained teachers in elementary schools increased from 186 in 1870 to 527 in 1892 (*Reports, Education Department* 1870, 1892). An important measure for improving the quality of the denominational system was improvement in the number and quality of teachers trained. In December 1882, the Department of Education began to set common examinations for training college students for the first time (Cundall 1914: 34; *Report, Education Department* 1882-83: xi). The pupil teacher examinations were also reorganized and run on a collective basis through centres. Untrained teachers with more than ten years' service were allowed to head schools after they had passed examinations set by the Department of Education (Cundall 1914: 25-28; White 1977: 45, 46). All these moves to improve efficiency and quality resulted in increased recurrent costs. In addition, up to this point teachers were still without a pension scheme (Goulbourne 1988: 97).

While in the 1830s and 1840s the English concept of education was that it was a church function, by the 1880s that thinking had changed. Education was now seen as the responsibility of the government, not the churches. Schools were increasingly being financed by local government as far as recurrent costs were concerned and new schools were built by these local authorities (Aldrich 1982: 83). The shift of responsibility for education in England from church to state also had its impact, for similar shifts began to take place in Jamaica.

The denominations began to find it increasingly difficult to meet the recurrent cost of an improved and expanded elementary system. Ecumenical cooperation could have alleviated this burden by the voluntary amalgamation of small uneconomical schools in the same locality run by different denominations. However, the denominational rivalry was such that they appeared to prefer to hand over the system to the state than to cooperate with each other.

The number and location of the schools built by the denominations reflected not only demand and need by the children served, but also denominational rivalry. Education was a major means of proselytization. Neither the Negro Education Grant nor the state support from the Assembly had been able to control this factor. By 1895 there were 962 schools serving 99,790 children, an average of 104 pupils per school (*Blue Books* 1895). To approximate the magnitude of the economic error committed by the denominations, one can compare the number of schools in 1895 with the number in 1984. In 1984, there were 800 primary and all-age schools catering to 412,000 children in Jamaica. During the ninety-year period, the number of schools had declined by 15 per cent, although the school age population had increased by more than 412 per cent. Yet, in 1895 there were many children not enrolled in schools. The recurrent cost of so many small uneconomic units was high. In many villages there were several small schools each belonging to different denominations but, apparently, the denominations could not agree to remedy this by themselves.

It is against this background that the educational reforms of 1892 must be understood. The denominational system of education was transferred to the government and became the state system of elementary education by the Education Law of 1892. The essential elements of the reform could be summarized as follows:

(a) the denominations would continue to own their schools and would be partially responsible for their maintenance;
(b) boards of management would be established for each school which would hire and dismiss teachers;
(c) the denominations would continue to manage the schools;

(d) government would meet all recurrent costs for providing elementary education;
(e) students' fees would be abolished in elementary schools;
(f) government would impose an education tax which would generate revenue to compensate for fees; and
(g) the Department of Education was to assume responsibility for the curriculum and the financing of education including teachers' salaries.

The colony was enjoying a period of economic prosperity and, therefore, the state was in a position to take over the recurrent financing of the denominational schools without doing anything about its more serious weakness – duplication of schools in small villages.

The growth and improvement of elementary education between 1865 and 1892 is not accounted for solely by state support for the denominational system. As important was the state of the general economy, especially as this impacted on the black population. Morant Bay was a small settlers' rebellion. Crown Colony government immediately set out to address their concerns. These included communications, education, health, the administration of justice, and land tenure.

Eisner points out that "the importance of the new constitution lay in the government's attitude in the wider sense; its encouragement of peasant expansion, protection of their interests – as in the struggle with the banana monopoly – and the provision of public works" (Eisner 1961: 235). She further stated that the rise of the peasants after the Morant Bay Rebellion was greater than population growth and employment opportunities in other sectors (Eisner 1961: 221).

Probably of greater significance was the fact that increasingly, they broke into the export trade. The shift in peasant production is shown by comparing the pattern of production in 1850 and 1890.

	1850	**1890**
Ground provision	83%	74%
Exports	11%	23%
Animal products	6%	3%

Eisner reported that the peasants' share of the total export market increased fourfold between 1850 and 1890 and that ground provision accounted for 55 per cent of the total agricultural output (Eisner 1961: 168, 235). The black peasantry moved into the export of banana, coffee, logwood, arrowroot and other minor crops. The first export of bananas was in 1869. From the 1870s, bananas increasingly supplanted sugar as the major export crop. By 1910 it accounted for half the total value of exports (Eisner 1961: 238). Because its production was less capital and more labour intensive than sugar, small farmers were able to participate in export production.

The general economy also benefited from the recovery of the sugar industry during this period, especially because of the export of sugar and rum to the American market. While its fortunes have waxed and waned in different periods, sugar has always been an important plank of the Jamaican economy. Buoyancy in this sector had an overall positive effect on the economic life of the colony.

At the same time that sugar was recovering and black people were increasingly engaged in peasant farming and small scale export production, migration to Central America became a significant factor of the labour scene. Eisner reported that net departures totalled 23,791 between 1881 and 1890, and 43,438 between 1891 and 1910 (Eisner 1961: 147-51). These were mainly black males seeking work in the building of Central American railroads and the Panama Canal.

It is in this economic context that the planting interests began to advocate the use of female teachers in schools instead of male teachers. The availability of labour for work on plantations was a cause of concern especially in parishes where there were large numbers of small settlers (Newton 1984: 103). The planting interests had always been concerned about any development that appeared to decrease the availability of cheap agricultural labour. An increase in the numbers engaged in peasant farming and migration of men to Central America signalled danger in the minds of these interests.

Walcott of St Mary confronted the issues squarely in a debate in the Legislative Council in 1900 and is on record as stating that "men as a rule were not good teachers. Women were the heaven ordained teachers, a fact which had been realized in other countries. At least 2/4 of the schools of the country ought to be under the control of efficient women teachers. The sooner they utilized the best female talent available and the sooner they would free a large portion of the male teachers so that they might occupy themselves in productive industry, the better for all concerned" (*Proceedings, JLC* 1900: 182). Productive industry in 1900 meant only agriculture or trades.

It is important to take note of the state of the island's economy during the 1890s. In 1892, in his address to the Legislative Council the governor said: "I am glad to inform you that the island is in a sound and prosperous condition". He continued to itemize the areas which reflected this prosperity:

(a) increase in exports;
(b) import duty collections exceeded the estimate and were above the

amount collected in the previous year;

(c) increase in the banana trade (18 per cent);

(d) increase in the export of oranges (13 per cent);

(e) increase in the export of sugar, rum, logwood and coffee; and

(f) estimated surplus in revenue of £56,992 sterling.

By 1897 conditions had changed. The governor, in his address to the Council stated that in the previous year there was

> brisk business, increase of exports and imports, and marked increase in the amount of deposits in the Savings Bank. This state of prosperous progress has received a temporary break ... the rapid decrease in the value of logwood ... the export of coffee, cocoa and hides has diminished ... while the price of the two former has been considerably lower... the serious fall in the price of sugar and rum and the contracted market for the latter so hampered estate owners that the labour bill was reduced to the lowest limits (*Proceedings, JLC* 1897: 2).

The situation remained unchanged in 1898. In March of that year the governor stated in the Council: "I deeply regret that after a series of prosperous years the island has suffered during the past 12 or 15 months from a number of unfortunate circumstances which have combined to effect a marked change for the worse in the prosperity of the community... The change in the circumstances of the people has had its natural effect on the public revenue" (*Proceedings, JLC* 1898: 3).

In 1899 a change for the better occurred. The governor's tone in his address to the Council that year was more optimistic (*Proceedings, JLC* 1898-99: 3):

> There have recently been signs of a distinct improvement in the conditions of the colony... the tide of prosperity which had so long been on the ebb, has reached low water mark, and is about to turn and flow again. During the later months of 1898 and the months of the present year already passed, not only have the trade and revenue improved but there are indications of a more hopeful spirit among the people. Some parishes indeed may be said to be already prosperous... I believe the outlook is brightening and that the time has come when the leaders and teachers of the people may bid them cease despondency, and encourage them to look forward to the gradual return to former prosperity.

The denominations gave up, or lost, effective control of the elementary schools at the time when they had been most successful in delivering a reasonable quality of elementary education to a majority of the black children whose parents were now eagerly seeking it for them. The root of their financial problems lay in rapid recent capital expansion, a pattern of capitalization which maximized recurrent costs, and increased demands by a better qualified teaching force. The denominations had over-extended themselves in the period 1867-90. To retain control of their schools, ecumenical cooperation was mandatory, but the politics of denominational rivalry dictated capitulation to the state as the most convenient path, the line of least resistance (*Proceedings, JLC* 1898-99: 53, 72).

The government had taken over the education system during a time of economic prosperity in which it had surplus revenue. In taking over denominational education, it had abolished fees and, accordingly, introduced free elementary education.

The decision to examine the economy and efficiency of the recently acquired elementary system came during the period of economic recession which was approximately five years after the take-over. The Lumb Commission did address the problem of the duplication of schools and recommended the amalgamation of many small schools in the same district. The denominations insisted that where denominational schools were amalgamated, the single school that was created would be a government school. Actually, the process of amalgamation seems to have started before the Lumb Commission had reported (Gordon 1968: 116). Table 3.10 shows a significant reduction in the number of schools between 1897 and 1898. It would also appear that the decision to amalgamate the schools was designed to produce a more efficient system rather than to reduce government expenditure in 1899. In the debate on the Lumb Commission and on the specific question of amalgamation, Burke from St Thomas pointed out that the Council had voted "the whole of the previous year's Education vote save about £4000" (*Proceedings, JLC* 1898-99: 193). He was making the point that there was no urgent financial reason to close schools in particular areas where local problems dictated additional time before the implementation of the amalgamation decision.

In the 1898 debate on the estimates in the Legislative Council, a motion was moved to reduce the education vote and teaching salaries by 10 per cent. The motion was defeated (*Proceedings, JLC* 1898: 215). Charges were made that it was a move to pressure the Department of Education to work out a scheme for reducing educational expenditure. In the debate on this motion, several points were raised in defense of education and teachers' salaries. These included the following:

(a) that if government's intention was to reduce expenditure, then several other areas had to be included, not only education;
(b) that the amalgamation of elementary schools in some areas could result in significant savings; and
(c) that no decisions should be taken since the issue of reduction or

educational expenditure was receiving attention from the Lumb Commission.

The Superintendent Inspector, Mr Capper, and the governor were strong advocates of the latter position (*Proceedings, JLC* 1898: 217-19).

Harsh criticisms were made of teachers' colleges. Burke maintained that expenditure on teacher training was needless because many teachers were not practising as teachers (*Proceedings, JLC* 1898: 220). He advocated that the government's guarantee for annual grants to Mico end in 1899 and not be renewed. Palache (*Proceedings, JLC* 1898: 210) was of the view that the large expenditure on teacher training was not justified by the results obtained. Anti-denominational sentiments emerged, but it was pointed out that the denominational colleges were the least costly of the existing colleges.

In the debate on the estimates in 1899, the mood was different. The optimistic note sounded by the governor in respect of the economy was reflected in the attitude of the members to reduction in educational expenditure. There was a general consensus among the elected members against reductions in the education vote (*Proceedings, JLC* 1898-99: 128). The Colonial Secretary was of the view that the savings to be derived from the amalgamation of schools were sufficient and, therefore, further reductions were not warranted (*Proceedings, JLC* 1898-99: 128).

Financial reasons were not cited as the grounds for withdrawing government grants to denominational colleges which trained male teachers – Fairfield and Calabar. Economic factors relating to the supply of agricultural labour did contribute to the proposal to train women instead of men as teachers. Economic factors also provided the context and the climate in which the decision was made to discontinue the support of denominational training of male teachers. As such, they provided the opportunity for the closure of these colleges. However, economic and financial considerations were not cited and were not the immediate reasons for the decision that was made.

Political Factors

The post-Emancipation period began with the planter class doing everything in its power to try to perpetuate the concepts and conditions of slavery in the free society. The planters remained the visible and vocal opponents of the ex-slaves (Jacobs 1973: 62). The allies of the Blacks had been the non-conformist churches through their missionaries and the imperial government. They had championed the Emancipation movement and continued to assist the ex-slaves in their transition to freedom. In other words, the protagonists of the battle over the abolition of slavery continued to fight each other in the establishment of the free society.

The reactionary planters controlled the Assembly. They formed what has been referred to as the "Country Party". They were opposed by the "Town Party" which consisted mainly of coloured men and Jews (Campbell 1963: 10, 14). It is these men who voiced, in the Assembly, the progressive views for changes proposed by the governor and the missionaries. While this is a simplification of the situation, it gives a rough picture of the relationships. Under the old Constitution, while the governor was powerful and could veto bills from the Assembly, he was constrained by having no power to initiate financial provisions. Through its control of finances, the Assembly could frustrate the governor (Heuman 1981: 149).

Two great fears dominated the period 1834 to 1865. First, Blacks feared the reintroduction of slavery through annexation of Jamaica by the United States. In 1847, Hector Michell, Custos of Kingston, through his newspaper advocated annexation and Sir Charles Grey, Governor, spoke in 1848 of a sessionist movement in Jamaica (Jacobs 1973: 76). Jacobs points out that influential politicians in the USA, including Senator Hannegan, chairman of the Foreign Relations Committee and Jefferson Davis, later president of the Confederacy, interpreted emancipation of slaves in the Caribbean as part of a British expansionist scheme to surround Florida with a cordon of Negro freedmen (Jacobs 1973: 77). It would appear that after the annexation of Texas in 1846, some Jamaican planters flirted with annexation as a means of restoring slavery. This fear – or hope – was finally laid to rest with the Civil War in the USA which ended, coincidentally, in 1865.

The second fear on the part of Whites and some Browns was that Blacks would seize political power leading to Jamaica becoming another Haiti (Jacobs 1973: 88; Black 1958: 205; Patterson 1967: 277; Allen 1904). The Assembly made sure that Blacks would not acquire political power by democratic means by restricting the franchise to vote and putting even more stringent requirements on conditions to be satisfied by representatives (Heuman 1981: 104, 116-33; Curtin 1955: 175-81). For Blacks to acquire political power, rebellion was the most likely means.

The foregoing gives a rough idea of the political climate of the period 1834-65. White men (planters) fighting white men – missionaries and colonial administrators – over freedom for Blacks. Coloured men and Jews were caught in the middle but, on the whole, supported the governor and the nonconformist churches.

In the power relations of the time, it was no accident that the denominations were given the franchise to establish education for the Blacks. They, not the planters and the Assembly (the state), were the allies of the British government and the Blacks.

To the Blacks and some churchmen, the denominational system was established to consolidate Emancipation. It was part of the institutional infrastructure of freedom that had to be established. Education had to be inspired by an ideology of redemption and liberation. It had to provide the basis for the social, economic and political progress of the black man in a free society.

More than a century before, the endowed system had been established with a similar redemption ideology (Gordon 1963: 15). Its aim was to redeem and restore poor Whites who had become trapped in the colony. In the last decades of the eighteenth century and the pre-Emancipation period, this redemption was extended to Mulattoes and Jews when those groups demanded their civil rights.

The planters opposed the denominational system in terms of its curriculum content. They advocated agricultural and industrial education. They established industrial schools to rival the elementary schools (Heuman 1981: 138; Gordon 1963: 59, 71). These schools were provided for children who came under the care of the state. The missionaries and Blacks avoided agricultural education because it conflicted with their redemption or liberation ideology, for the possibilities of social and economic progress through this type of education were minimal (Campbell 1963: 118-20). The protagonists of slavery fought the battle of freedom by taking different postures on the type of education which they considered appropriate for Blacks. The battle continued until the Morant Bay Rebellion.

Crown colony government changed the power relations in the colony. At first sight, it may appear that the voluntary surrender of the limited sovereignty enjoyed by the colony under the old constitution represented a victory for the Blacks since the great benefactors, the imperial government, now ruled directly through the new crown colony constitution. The reforms that took place under the first crown colony governor, Sir John Peter Grant, certainly would support such a position. These reforms included:

(a) the disestablishment of the Anglican Church as the state religion and the use of the monies saved for increased provision for education;
(b) the reform of the local government system replacing the vestries with municipal boards;
(c) reforms of the judicial system designed to eliminate colour and class prejudice;
(d) replacement of the militia with an expanded and reorganized police force; and

(e) improved social services including public health, education and communications (Black 1958: 104; Livingstone 1900: 84-86).

All of these reforms had beneficial effects on the lives of black people, and the improved public order that followed testified to acceptance by the large black population, that at last, the material conditions of their lives were being addressed in a meaningful and substantial way. The first decade of crown colony government brought about significant changes in areas that had been at the core of black discontentment. A delegation of Blacks from Kingston in 1884 stated to the Crossman Commission: "The system of education which has been steadily fostered by crown colony government will, in due time, produce an abundant harvest to repay for the systematic oversight, and raise up men fully qualified to take a lively interest in the welfare of their own land" (West Indies Royal Commission 1884).

In seeking to serve the interests of Blacks, crown colony government did not totally ignore the views of the planting interests that education offered to Blacks should have a strong vocational content. Domestic economy, agriculture and manual training were included in the 1867 reforms. Special grants were given for the teaching of needlework to girls and generous incentives were provided for schools devoting three hours per day to agricultural and industrial instruction. Children volunteering to receive such instruction were exempt from paying school fees. They received their education free.

It is interesting to note that vocational education for boys in elementary schools was the only aspect of the reforms that failed. Capper reviewing the 1867 reforms noted that reluctantly the government became "convinced by experience that it had been mistaken" in attempting to combine elementary education with actual labour, agricultural and manual (West Indies Royal Commission 1884). The main reason for this failure was parent resistance in spite of the incentive of free education if they accepted such instruction.

While black parents rejected vocational education for their sons, they accepted it for their daughters. Needlework became an accepted subject of the elementary school curriculum and enjoyed pupil and parent support. It would appear that the patriarchal values prevailing at the time and which facilitated parents accepting vocational education for their daughters were consistent with the stereotyped roles of wives and mothers. Needlework, however, provided a niche for female teachers in the elementary school. The larger schools were permitted to employ women teachers to teach sewing and infant care.

In the long term, however, crown colony government represented a victory for the reactionary planters who surrendered limited sovereignty for direct rule. Crown colony government did not employ blatant social practices of injustice, crude economic measures, crass manipulation of government machinery, or gross misuse of legal process as the planters had done. The measures adopted were far more sophisticated and subtle, but the ultimate ends served by crown colony government did not differ from those espoused by the studied attempt to transform the former slaves into voluntary agricultural labourers and tradesmen.

The important question becomes, what were the factors that could account for the change in the role of the crown in Jamaica from liberator, defender and benefactor of the Blacks to that of subjugator during the period 1865 to 1944? At least two factors seemed to have been at work. First, the Morant Bay Rebellion itself. Morant Bay authenticated the fear of the possibility of Blacks seizing power through rebellion and eliminating Whites (Black 1958: 205; Heuman 1981: 193).

It is quite interesting that all other West Indian colonies, except Barbados, voluntarily surrendered self-government and yielded to crown colony government as the Jamaican planters had done (Levy 1980: 156; Bolland 1977: 191, 192). Even in Barbados where the old constitution was retained, reforms which gave the governor greater powers in the affairs of the colony were agreed to. The Morant Bay Rebellion triggered constitutional changes, not only in Jamaica but throughout the British West Indian colonies. The immediate response was to ameliorate the conditions of the black population. But, the longer term problem was to ensure that *Haiti* did not occur in the English-speaking Caribbean.

Froude in his book, *The English in the West Indies* (1888), suggested that in the 1880s the view was that if the West Indian colonies were not to become so many Haitis, then it was essential to prevent the black population from obtaining any political power (Froude 1888: 81, 190, 191, 235, 261, 262). Morant Bay may have contributed to the evolution of such a general view.

Secondly, by the 1870s and 1880s Britain had developed new attitudes and views on the race question, consequent upon its experience in colonizing India and various countries in Africa. Jacobs points out that "there was an increasing tendency to regard the coloured races as requiring perpetual tutelage. It was in India that this attitude was most noticeable" (Jacobs 1973: 108; Froude 1888: 97). It would appear that in the process of the colonizing of non-white peoples globally, British attitudes and views concerning race had undergone changes that resulted in the black man being perceived more negatively in the 1880s and beyond, than was the case in the first half of the nineteenth century which was dominated by the liberal views of the evangelical humanitarians.

For whatever reason, it is with respect to race that crown colony government began to reverse trends that had emerged in the nineteenth century to that point. All the top posts in the civil service were placed in the hands of expatriate Whites (Jacobs 1973: 108). In the nineteenth century, up to 1865, several of the top posts were held by Jamaican Whites and by a few coloured men. Jordan had been Receiver General in the 1860s (Jacobs 1973: 105; Heuman 1981: 183). In fact, crown colony government re-established the pattern of going abroad to obtain managerial talent not only in the public, but the private sector as well. Morrison (West Indies Royal Commission 1884; *Jamaica Gazette* Feb. 1884), giving evidence to the Crossman Commission in 1884, stated:

> One of the saddest and most serious consequences of a system of official and political exclusion is the deprivation of the youth of the colony of all the incentive of healthy emulation, all the prospective prizes of honourable ambition. I am acquainted with the case of several parents who, having sent their sons to receive a liberal education at the Home public schools and universities, are filled with painful anxiety as to the future that would await their sons if they returned in the existing state of affairs, to fight the battle of life in their own country.

At the same time, crown colony government began to offer new educational opportunities to brown people via the creation of high schools through the reorganization of endowments. The result of this was to widen the cleavages between the Browns and the Blacks in the society. Jacobs observes: "this cleavage existed in slavery time, and it had been one of Jordan's greatest achievements to reduce its importance. We must not regard it as a mere survival, but rather a latent feeling reactivated by the new opportunities offered by crown colony rule to educate coloured people" (Jacobs 1973: 108). A question that cannot be ignored concerns the status of the non-conformist denominations when their long time ally – the crown – ruled directly. The simple answer is that by 1900, crown colony government had almost completely compromised its former allies. Jacobs puts the matter delicately and kindly, stating: "... under the crown colony system, the dissenting bodies lost much of their character as an opposition" (Jacobs 1973: 109).

The archenemies of the nonconformist denominations, the planters, were no longer in government. Even after 1884 when elected members were again admitted to the Legislative Council, their voice was not supreme. The Anglican church, the apologist of the planter class, had been disestablished. Religious discrimination which had been a grievous thorn to the dissenters no longer existed. Local government had been reformed so that the church wardens of the vestries no longer secured advantages for Anglicanism through the local government machinery. Grants to the denominations had increased significantly both to construct and maintain schools. Non-conformists were now on government boards and commissions; for example, they were represented on the Jamaica Schools Commission (King 1972: 64-65). Even when the state had taken over the recurrent financing of the denominational system in 1892, it had left them with ownership of the property and responsibility for the day to day management as well as the authority to command teachers to perform duties outside of the schoolroom (*Proceedings, JLC* 1892-93). By 1900, the fire of missionary fervour on behalf of the black man had been substantially quenched by the waters of benevolence of crown colony government. If the last decades of the eighteenth century saw the lighting of this fire which flamed furiously in the first half of the nineteenth century, the last decade of that century witnessed the last flicker of that flame.

It is in this context that the formation of the Jamaica Union of Teachers (JUT) in 1894 has to be understood. Goulbourne points out that the 1892 reforms which established the state system of elementary education left the teacher at the mercy of the Inspector from the Department of Education to determine his salary (Goulbourne 1988: 97). It gave the manager, the minister of religion, the power to dismiss him on grounds unrelated to his professional duties. No provisions were made to provide for his old age. In addition, the governor and others in the debate in 1892 had cited incompetent schoolmasters as one of the chief reasons for not considering compulsory education at that time (*Proceedings, JLC* 1892: 93).

Some schoolmasters spoke out in defense of their own competence and urged their colleagues to come together to form a union to defend their rights. In that act, they raised the spectre of black political power. Even of greater significance is the fact that they raised it against the state and the church, their former allies. Letters written by teachers appeared in the press which took issue with the governor and the Superintendent Inspector of Schools, Mr Capper (Goulbourne 1988: 100). Clearly, their action signalled the possibility of the predominantly male teaching force becoming a militant group of Blacks in the society. While the public agitation leading to the formation of the JUT manifested some militant postures, the newly formed union took every precaution to avoid projecting a confrontational stance.

Before examining the immediate political circumstances surrounding the closure of the male denominational colleges, one further element needs to be discussed: that of the advocacy for female teachers in elementary schools.

From the end of the 1870s the training of female teachers became an issue which persisted until the turn of the century. One argument for female teachers centred on the questions of neglect and injustice. Dr Robert Lowe, black activist of the late nineteenth century supported this argument (*Reports and Statistics Congregation of United Brethren* 1895: 14). Thomas Capper, Inspector of Schools, took a similar position stating that:

> There can be no question of the immense advantage to education that would be secured by the establishment of such an institution; and it would be some slight reparation for the unintentional but grave injustice which has hitherto not only passed over girls entirely in the assistance extended to higher education, especially the training of teachers, but has deprived them of the equal share in the benefits of many educational endowments which the founders intended that they should enjoy (*Report, Education Department* 1882-83: 141).

The somewhat belated recognition of the gender inequalities of the educational system, especially in teacher education, enjoyed wide public support resulting in a petition in 1883 signed by most custodes and several leading ministers of religion requesting the governor to establish a government training college for females. The first success of this movement was the establishment of the Shortwood Teachers' College in 1885.

In 1890, the Legislative Council voted an annual grant to Mico for the training of male teachers (*Proceedings, JLC* 1891-92: 17). Mico declined the grant, unless the government gave the college a guarantee that it would continue for at least seven years. That Mico could have taken such a position would seem to suggest that there was cause for uncertainty. The government had closed its training college for male teachers in 1890, and transferred the first and second year students to Mico. The Legislative Council debate in 1891 on the subject of the guarantee is instructive in respect of the arguments for and against women teachers.

Colonel Ward and several elected members were opposed to giving Mico any such guarantee on the basis that the government should not commit itself to the continued preparation of male teachers but should be expanding the efforts to prepare female teachers (*Proceedings, JLC* 1891-92: 17-18). Solomon took the position that he would not object to the guarantee if Mico agreed to train forty men and twenty women (*Proceedings, JLC* 1891-92: 18).

The arguments advanced for female teachers could be summarized as follows:

1. Fifty to 60 per cent of the teachers in the United States of America were female and that system of women teachers could be adopted in Jamaica.

2. Women were found to be better teachers than men in elementary schools.
3. It was cheaper to employ women. In the USA they were half the cost of men.
4. The tone and morale of schools run by women would be higher than those run by men.
5. Schools run by women would be more efficient.
6. Women were more honest.
7. Men were leaving teaching and seeking employment in other spheres.

The defence by the Inspector of Schools, Mr Capper, of the practice of hiring male teachers deserves to be quoted in full (*Proceedings, JLC* 1891-92: 17-18). He found himself

> ... in accord with members as to the advisability of inducing women to act as teachers. Indeed, he felt strongly on the subject but still ... could not go faster than was practicable ... In the first place there was great difficulty in getting properly qualified candidates to enter as teachers but this difficulty was disappearing year by year and now they were coming up to the standard which was fixed as the minimum considered desirable. Another difficulty was that after they had finished their training it was well nigh impossible to find schools for them with the system at present in existence. They could not force female teachers on managers who did not want them; they could only persuade them that they were better than male teachers and this they were slowly doing. Then female teachers require more looking after than men. When male teachers went to a school the managers left him to find his own accommodation – they could not do this with female teachers who required some comfort and care as regards their arrangements for living ... still the number of male teachers turned out were not sufficient for the needs of the colony. All students leaving the college were snapped up directly they left by the schools in the country and as a general rule they did good work. When a man became a teacher the probability was that he entered the profession for life – at any rate the vast majority gave several years to the work ...There was a rule in the Department that the teacher who was convicted of immorality was not further recognized and it was very probable that some of those teachers who sought employment in other spheres were men who had been thus dismissed.

One aspect of Colonel Ward's response to Mr Capper proved to be prophetic and is worth noting: "As to the objection of the Inspector of Schools that there were difficulties finding female teachers sufficiently advanced in education to take their places in training colleges, he would say that females seeing no possibility in getting employment in the past have not prepared themselves but if they saw the possibilities of employment many would so prepare themselves" (*Proceedings, JLC* 1891-92: 18).

He further claimed that managers preferred men because they could use them to preach and perform other duties.

The Colonial Secretary and the president both supported the Inspector of Schools. They agreed that female teachers were superior, but claimed to be impotent to do anything about the present system which was prejudiced against employing women teachers (*Proceedings, JLC* 1891-92: 18). Those claiming inability to do anything about the existing system were the most powerful personages in the colony as far as politics and schools were concerned – the Superintendent Inspector, the Colonial Secretary and the governor.

Mico finally got their guarantee, but this debate of 1891 is typical of the strong arguments by the elected – and some nominated – members of the Legislative Council for the training and employment of female teachers. The argument at that stage was no longer one of inequality and neglect, female teachers in equal numbers to male teachers; it was female teachers instead of male teachers. This argument accepted that teachers would come from the black population but advocated that the opportunity should be given to the woman and not the man.

The point to be noted is that up to that time, the colonial administrators, while giving verbal consent to the argument for female teachers, did not take any positive action to translate this argument into reality. They had made concessions by establishing Shortwood and closing the government college for male teachers in Spanish Town, but this had left the balance in favour of male teachers.

The elected members continued to advocate for the use of women teachers in the schools, despite the setback in the 1891 debate. They maintained a clear vision, not only that women should replace men as teachers but about what black men should be educated to do.

The immediate events leading to the closure of Fairfield and Calabar could be summarized as follows:

1. The Lumb Commission was appointed in December 1897 during the middle of the economic recession.
2. It reported in December 1898.
3. After publication of the report numerous petitions were submitted to the Legislative Council in 1899.
4. The Council appointed a Select Committee to consider both the report and the petitions.
5. Bishop Nuttall submitted a memorandum, more or less giving the response of the Commission to issues raised by the petitions.
6. The Legislative Council then debated the report of the Select Committee and that of the Lumb Commission. This debate went on until June 1899.

7. The Department of Education, during and after the debate, set about implementing both the accepted policy recommendations and matters it considered to be consequential to the new directions.

Several recommendations of the Commission were not agreed on or accepted at that time. These included:

(a) compulsory primary education for all children 6-12 years of age;
(b) lowering of the school leaving age to 12 years;
(c) fixed salaries for teachers;
(d) higher salaries for male head teachers than for female head teachers;
(e) abolition of scholarships;
(f) award of the Jamaica Scholarship every three years; and
(g) drastic reductions in expenditure on secondary education.

The commission's recommendations on the amalgamation of schools, closure of the University College, and curriculum reform in teachers' colleges and elementary schools were accepted and implemented (*Report, Education Department* 1899-1900: 359, 377, 378).

The essence of the curriculum reform was for greater emphasis on agriculture and industrial instruction. Successful implementation in the elementary schools required teachers trained in agriculture and manual instruction. The Department of Education argued that Fairfield and Calabar could not meet the requirements of the new curriculum approved for training colleges (*Report, Education Department* 1899-1900: 360):

> It is not a reflection upon their work that the government does not continue the maintenance grants. It is believed that with the shortened course of training, the Mico will sufficiently meet the needs of this country in the training of young men to be teachers, and that the work can be done at the Mico more effectively than at either Fairfield or Calabar. For example, the Mico, with its extensive grounds can give training in agricultural instruction which would be impossible at Calabar, and because of its connection with the Kingston Manual Training School it can give instruction in manual training which would be impracticable at Fairfield. The Mico is capable of expansion and when there comes to be a greater demand for additional trained young men than the Mico can now supply, arrangements can be made for an increase of students to be trained at that college.

Having extolled the place of Mico relative to the other male colleges, the department proceeded to reduce its enrolment from 80 to 60 students at the very time Fairfield and Calabar were being closed (*Report, Education Department* 1899-1900: 360).

Goulbourne in investigating the circumstances leading to the formation of the JUT and the involvement of teachers in politics in colonial Jamaica came to the conclusion that the move to make elementary school teaching a feminine occupation "is suggestive of a deliberate attempt to keep salaries down, release men for agricultural work, since agricultural labour was perceived by the less enlightened planters who were well represented in the colonial state as one of the crucial problems of the period. Another reason for such action many also have been to undermine the militancy of a political occupation" (Goulbourne 1988: 106). It would appear that it is this latter reason which was the crucial factor that changed the government's position from defence of male teachers in 1891 to the withdrawal of grants to denominational colleges training male teachers, recognizing fully that this would reduce the number of males being trained for the schoolroom.

Male teachers were not without defenders in 1899. In the Legislative Council debate on grant-in-aid in education, questions were raised about the cost of training female teachers at Shortwood. It was claimed that each student trained at Shortwood cost £40 annually – the highest cost among the colleges (*Proceedings, JLC* 1898-99: 130). Mr Capper stated that the Department of Education "had been originally disposed to close the college altogether as being too expensive but a number of Ministers of Religion and other influential persons in Kingston thought that the institution had done good work and should not be abandoned. They pressed their view upon the government and offered to undertake to carry on the college for £40 per student inclusive of everything" (*Proceeedings, JLC* 1898-99: 130. The Colonial Secretary supported the Inspector of Schools. He stated that Archbishop Nuttall had represented the case of the college and claimed that closure would damage education to some extent and that it was desirable to have female teachers and to keep the college open (*Proceedings, JLC* 1898-99: 130).

Dr Johnson opposed the Inspector of Schools and the Colonial Secretary (*Proceedings, JLC* 1898-99: 130). Essentially he repeated much of the argument they had used in 1891. The essence of his argument could be summarized as follows:

1. He saw no arguments to prove the usefulness of Shortwood.
2. He failed to see openings for female teachers in the schools.
3. The demand was for male teachers and until there were different circumstances in the schools the situation would continue.
4. Certified female teachers taught under provisionally appointed male teachers.
5. Men could be used as catechists on Sundays.

Dr Johnson was the lone voice in support of male teachers. Dixon from St Elizabeth pronounced the benediction on that debate when he stated "they wanted women teachers and if those they had failed, they must get a fresh lot" (*Proceedings, JLC* 1898-99: 130). The only concession made to Dr Johnson was that the vote for Shortwood and the number of students were reduced slightly.

The most significant aspect of this debate was that the colonial administrators had changed sides relative to the position they had taken in 1891. They found themselves arguing against the very positions they had stated in 1891. Now they were unable to resist the representations of the Archbishops, other ministers of religion and influential persons from Kingston for the training of female teachers. The colonial administrators seemed to give the impression that they were powerless to do anything about the position they were accepting as the basis for their action. The crucial question is: why had they shifted their position on male teachers between 1891 and 1899?

The department decided to discontinue government financial assistance to Fairfield and Calabar. The denominations decided to close the colleges on the grounds that they could not make up the deficit that would be created by the loss of the government grants.

The denominational system met its recurrent expenses from three sources: (a) student fees; (b) missionary grants; and (c) government subsidy. In 1889, the income and expenses of the Fairfield College were as follows:

Government aid	—	£2,700
Fees	—	545
Grant from England	—	146
Total income	—	3,391
Salaries	—	2,825
Buildings	—	539
Total expenditure	—	£3,364

The withdrawal of government aid would make it difficult for the college to pay salaries (Hastings and McLeary 1979: 92).

There is no evidence that either the Baptists or the Moravians protested the decision to withdraw the grants or of the basis on which that action was justified. Nor is there any evidence that they put up any alternative to closure. Calabar was located one mile from both Mico and the Kingston Manual Training School. The limitations of its facilities could have been overcome by collaborative arrangements with neighbouring institutions, just as the department had proposed for Mico with manual instructions. Moreover, the curriculum being introduced in the colleges was precisely that which the denominations had fought against for sixty years. The Jamaica Baptist Union did petition the Council protesting the lowering of standards in teachers' colleges, but did not support this with any action (*Proceedings, JLC* 1899-1900: 53).

Hastings and MacLeary agreed that the closure of Fairfield was not adequately explained in the records. They state: "...the enforced closure of Fairfield is still one of the unsolved mysteries of the Moravian church in Jamaica. Was it really due to financial difficulties through which the government was then passing? ... had the Moravian church or Fairfield fallen into the 'black book' of the government? Did the church yield too easily and readily to the demands of the government? Or was Fairfield closed in the interest of Mico?" (Hastings and McLeary 1979: 92).

At the same time that Fairfield was closed, the Moravian church established theological training in the West Indies to train native ministers of religion. They bought the Mico college in Antigua for that purpose. The Leeward Islands students at that institution were transferred to Mico in Jamaica to complete their training (Cundall 1914: 27). Fairfield was considered for the location of ministerial training. Apparently it lost the contest for both ministerial and teacher training. The point being made is that there is some evidence to suggest that the Moravians, at that time, were shifting their emphasis to ministerial rather that teacher training (Hark and Westphal 1904).

Also there may have been some disenchantment between the church and the college. Pastor C.S. Smyth of the Fairfield Church lamented the fact that the young men in training at the college were not looked upon as members of the congregation, but as visitors (Reports and Statistics, Congregation of United Brethren 1895: 25): "the consequence is they naturally lose that regard they ought to have for the authority and discipline of the church, and are in some cases at least, a direct stumbling block in the way of the young people of the congregation who, seeing the slack discipline and careless behaviour of some of them, become very heady and obstinate when reproved" (*Handbook of Jamaica* 1882: 372). This statement is not far removed from some of those made by elected members of the Legislature. Control of these young black men seemed to have been a problem. They were not following the lines laid down for them. They may even have been talking back.

Up to 1887, the Calabar institution was located in Rio Bueno, Trelawny. In 1887, it was transferred to East Queen Street in Kingston. Law 39 of 1887 recorded the purpose of Calabar College as that of the education of Baptist ministers and also of day school teachers of any Christian denomination (*Handbook of Jamaica* 1882: 372). In 1900, the same year in which it closed the division for training teachers, the General Committee of Calabar College decided that the East Queen

Street site was not suitable for the purpose of the college. In April 1901, acting through trustees, it purchased Chetolah Park in Hannah Town as the new site of the college. After constructing appropriate buildings, the college was relocated at Chetolah Park in 1904. The purpose of the new Calabar College was stated "as a Theological College for the education and training of students for the Pastoral Office in Baptist Churches in Jamaica for missionary work in connection with the Baptist denomination ... for the education and training of students not specially intended for the pastoral office and whether of the Baptist denomination or of any other Christian denomination ...." (*Trust Deed of Calabar College* 1904). In 1912, after appropriate buildings had been erected, the Baptists opened Calabar High School for boys on the new Chetolah park site (*Handbook of Jamaica* 1939: 365).

It would appear that the Baptist involvement in teacher training was related to providing teachers for its elementary schools. Following the transfer of elementary education to the state in 1892, the Baptists, by 1900 were reconsidering and refocusing their involvement in education. Were they still committed to teacher training, the new spacious site at Chetolah Park would allow them to overcome the technical difficulties raised by the Department of Education concerning its East Queen Street location. Instead, they established a boys' high school as the other part of its education programme on the new site. The lack of opposition by the Baptists in 1899 and 1900 to the withdrawal of the grant to the teacher training division of the college seems to be related to the fact that they were considering moving out of teacher training and into high school education; they were shifting their educational involvement.

The JUT was silent on both the withdrawal of the grants by the government and the closure of the colleges by the denominations. This was in sharp contrast to their opposition to aspects of the Lumb Commission and proposed changes to the Elementary Education Bill in the 1898-99 session. They had petitioned the Council against compulsory education and the lowering of the school-leaving age recommended by Lumb. They had opposed the reimposition of fees for children under six years on the grounds that the education tax introduced in 1892, when free elementary education was established, was intended to cover the fees of children of that age also (*Proceedings, JLC* 1899-1900: 32, 78). A deputation waited on the Select Committee to put forward its view on both matters (*Proceedings, JLC* 1899-1900: 210). It could have been that the lack of resistance from the denominations, and the technical reasons advanced for the withdrawal of the grants by the Department of Education induced silence on the part of the JUT. If the decision was acceptable to the Moravians and the Baptists, why should they protest?

Probably of greater importance was the trust that the leadership of the union had in Crown Colony government. In 1903, the acting president, and one of the founders of the Union, stated in his address to Conference: "I can believe that our authorities are handicapped for want of funds ... but ... we will never believe that they will wilfully hurt the men and women whose assistance and intelligent cooperation are indispensable if improvements are to be carried out in the material as well as the mental and moral development of our people ..." (*Annual Report, JUT* 1903: 8)

But there was yet another factor related to the colonial administrators' willingness to shift elementary school teaching in favour of females. This factor was never revealed publicly but forms part of the confidential records of the Colonial Office. Female teachers would help to loosen the hold of the churches on the newly inaugurated state system of elementary education. While the state now controlled the elementary school system the churches, through the clergy, managed the schools. While the state now bore the cost and determined policy, the churches still had significant influence in running the system. The acquisition of power and influence from the churches by the state was not clear-cut, simple nor easy.

In a letter to the Colonial Secretary in November 1899 Capper wrote:

> When the Education law was passed in 1892 I hoped that the Board of Education formed under that Law would cooperate with me in an endeavour to extinguish schools which obviously did not benefit the cause of education but rather the reverse. I have been disappointed in my expectations. The clerical members of the Board (amongst whom I do not count Reverend M Simms, as he does not take a sectarian or ecclesiastical view of such matters) attend with considerable regularity and are often unanimously in favour of recognition of schools considered unnecessary by the Department, and unanimously against the consideration of the question of striking off schools considered by the Department to be superfluous.

Previously, in a confidential letter in January 1899, Capper had complained to the Colonial Office that many of the teachers in the schools considered superfluous by the department were cathecists for the various denominations. Further, that the stipend from their work as cathecists could not sustain them without their salary as teachers. The churches were against the closure of superfluous schools because it would affect their ecclesiastical arrangements in the communities involved. Capper was also critical of the quality of the teaching of teacher/cathecists in the schools.

The essence of Capper's complaints was that the churches were using the school system to subsidize their ecclesiastical endeavours and for that reason obstructing the department from executing necessary economies in the restructuring of the newly acquired state system of elementary schooling. It is amusing that ecumenical unity and regular attendance of Education Board meetings, two virtues not commonly known among the clergy, should cause the Director of Education such discomfort. Neither was indirect subsidy of denominational endeavours by the state new. Clearly, by 1899 the colonial officials saw no further usefulness in that subsidy. However, the minister/manager and the teacher/cathecist were proving difficult nuts to crack in the state controlled school system. The state bureaucracy was finding it difficult to deal with these men. Women as teachers was one of the means by which the churches' hegemony over the school system could be broken.

To secure this end, the governor and Capper proposed that women teachers should be attracted into teaching by paying them the same salary as men. In correspondence with the Colonial Office, Capper, supported by the governor, set out this position very clearly. They did this in the context of taking issue with the recommendation from the Lumb Commission that women should be paid less than men. Capper wrote (Colonial Office Memorandum 1898):

> In paragraph 73 the Commission expresses the opinion in which I entirely concur that much school teaching should be done by women, and that a greater number of women should be employed as headteachers and assistants. The natural and it would seem the only way to secure this would be to make the profession attractive to women by increasing the possible salaries they can earn and offering them other advantages. What the Commission offers the best women teachers is –
>
> (1) a reduction of one-third of their present salaries as in the case of men;
> (2) a reduction of a third of the remainder because they are women;
> (3) the stoppage of the extra grant for sewing which they have hitherto enjoyed.
>
> There is considerable difficulty in getting suitable women candidates for training even now, and that this difficulty will be lessened by the Commission's proposal is more, I think, than the most sanguine can expect.

The Colonial Office considered the matters carefully and sanctioned the position taken by the governor and Capper. Female teachers in the Jamaican elementary school system, therefore, became one of the first groups of women anywhere to receive equal pay with men of the same qualification doing the same job. Further, the Department of Education offered large schools an additional teacher provided that teacher was female.

ANATOMY OF THE CLOSURE

It is important to examine the interrelationship between the major actors in the decision-making process relative to the closure of Fairfield and Calabar. This was a critical point in the shift in the institutional provision from favouring males to favouring females to be trained as elementary school teachers. By examining the interactions between the actors it should be possible to gain some insight into the changing nature of the old coalitions that were dissolving at the end of the nineteenth century and the new coalitions that were being formed in the Jamaican society at the beginning of the twentieth century.

Outspoken Planting Interests

For almost sixty years, the planting interests, especially through the elected members of the Legislative Assembly and later the Council, had been vocal and loud in their insistence on agricultural and industrial education for the black population. Their efforts were largely frustrated because they were not financing or controlling elementary education. The government began to fully finance and control elementary education in 1892. The economic crisis spanning 1897 to 1899 provided the welcome opportunity to restructure the curriculum of elementary schools and teachers' colleges accordingly. They had consistently and openly maintained that the socioeconomic place of the black man was as an agricultural labourer or tradesman. It was his labour that was required at low cost to maintain their wealth. For twenty years they had argued that since opportunity had to be given to train teachers it should be given to the black woman instead of the black man. They were not champions of women's rights. They simply intended to use the black woman against the black man and secure lower costs in the bargain by paying her less. For all the wrong reasons they were advocates of changes in the sexist structure of educational and employment opportunities at that time. They were, nonetheless, the pioneers of respectable employment for black women. By so doing, black men would be released for employment in the productive sector, the agricultural sector.

The Cunning Crown Colony Administrators

Since 1865, the crown colony administrators had tried to give the impression of being the impartial arbiters in deciding issues affecting different segments of the society. Increasingly, they had been tipping the scales in favour of the planting interests but that was never in the context of direct and open capitulation to pressure from that group. They were also sensitive to public opinion. While making concessions to the planters' interests on the question of using women instead of men as elementary school teachers, they had, by and large, defended men and the institutions training male teachers. That was up to 1894. But, with the formation of the JUT the potential of a militant group of organized educated black men could not be overlooked. Also the colonial administrator desired to have greater control of the newly acquired school system by loosening the close association between school work and church work by teachers. Yet, direct concession to the planting interests would require legislation dictating the closure of male institutions. This was undesirable. The curriculum reform of teacher education recommended by Lumb and the concentration of public protest on other aspects and recommendations of the commission provided the perfect opportunity for reductions to be made in the number of male teachers being trained without appearing to be accepting the arguments of the elected members who, no doubt, would support such action. The government must have known that withdrawal of the grants was tantamount to closure.

The sophistication of the department's actions deserves recognition. The reason given for withdrawal of the grant was technical, not political. It was the colleges' failure to meet new criteria, consequent upon reform. Public attention and protest were diverted to the closure of elementary schools as a result of amalgamation. Burke spoke about two hundred schools being on the "doomed list" of the department (*Proceedings, JLC* 1899-1900: 93). Economic and financial difficulties were widely accepted as the basis for the general reduction proposed in education. In any case, the department was not ordering closure. Instead, it pointed to the promise of the newly built and relocated Mico as being able to supply any future needs. The department's timing was perfect. It withdrew grants to denominational colleges training male teachers in the middle of the confusion and furore about amalgamation of elementary schools.

By a series of deft moves, the cunning crown colony administrators were simultaneously pursuing several ends. They were silently satisfying the planting interests, quietly subverting the possibility of a militant group of black men emerging in the colony, and covertly undermining the hold of the churches on the school system. To cap it all, the circumstances were so confusing and unclear that these moves by these crafty administrators went unchallenged.

The Retreating Churches

The nonconformist denominations had championed the cause of emancipation of the slaves and the rights of the Blacks in the free society, none more so than the Moravians and the Baptists. Since the establishment of crown colony government they had joined their allies, the crown, in providing elementary education of some quality. They assisted a few black men to rise to professional status and firmly established elementary schooling as the norm for children. In so doing, they had overextended themselves. This, ultimately, led to the surrender of finance and control of elementary schools to the state in 1892. Their association with the state had compromised their former glory which had been characterized by militancy. They were no longer the vigorous opponents of the planting interests. They were retreating from the educational success they had created but could not manage. So with almost willing compliance, they, and not the government, actually pulled the trigger of the rifle which slew the colleges that they had built and maintained for sixty years.

The Silent Union

The newly formed JUT, comprising mainly black men, had already developed a reputation for making its voice heard on matters affecting teachers and education. Trained in the context of missionary service, they were still possessed of faith in the ultimate goodness of those in authority. They were not, themselves, immediately involved. The withdrawal of the grants and the closure of the colleges represented decisions of the denominations and the Department of Education. There were no immediate victims knocking on the door of the union seeking assistance concerning their rights. Thus, the JUT apparently did not foresee the long term impact of these developments.

The Innocent Beneficiaries

Black women in Jamaica did not become teachers because they demanded such opportunity based on the improving performance in the school system. They did not actively seek to replace men as teachers. The women who would benefit and the colleges for female teachers that would grow as a result of the decision had done nothing to cause this outcome. They were the only innocents in the matter. Unknowingly, the black woman was being recruited by the ruling minority as an ally against the black man.

The only charge that could be made against the black woman was that by this alliance she was to become an accessory after the fact. This was through the socialization pattern which was to be established that eventually made teachers' colleges uncomfortable and skeptical of male students; a school system that would not be able to inspire black boys to achieve as much as black girls; and homes that would invest more in their girls than their boys.

From a position where it was very difficult to find suitably qualified women to be trained as teachers, the socialization pattern has been reversed to the point at which, ninety-three years later, it is difficult to find suitably qualified men to be trained as teachers.

The Absence of Conspiracy

There is no evidence of any active conspiracy between the actors involved in the decision to shift the institutional provision in favour of females. To date, there is no suggestion of any secret collaboration, no deceptive intrigues, no undercover deals, no sell-out involving planters, colonial officials, the clergy, the teachers' union or women. The decision to change the balance seems to have come about as a result of a concatenation of circumstances: persistent pursuit of self-interest, political decision making as it was directed by pressure groups and external influences, retreat from social responsibility, trusting silence, and unsuspecting co-option.

4

THE LONG-TERM IMPACT OF THE GENDER SHIFT

OUTCOME OF THE POLICY CHANGES

The restructuring of the denominational system of education in the last two decades of the nineteenth century set the stage for the change of primary school teaching from a masculine to a feminine occupation. The underlying reasons for this new policy direction were to:

(a) neutralize the potential development of a militant group of educated black men;
(b) lessen the influence of the church in the state controlled education system;
(c) keep black men as a cheap source of labour in the productive sector – agriculture;
(d) afford the black woman the status of social equal and not the black man; and
(e) reduce the cost of the teaching service by the lower salaries that could be commanded by women.

In part or in whole, all of these materialized in the early period of the twentieth century. Black militancy did not come from the formally educated black men but from Bedward, Marcus Garvey, the Rastafarian movement and the trade unions (Goulbourne 1988: 128-29). The Jamaica Union of Teachers, and elementary school teachers generally, were always caught in the middle between the cannons of respectability voiced by the profession and radical measures proposed by black activists in the face of oppression. Invariably the union trod the middle ground by offering critical social commentary on national issues, while leaving others to take mass action.

The churches' influence was eventually lessened in the state controlled system of elementary education, but ironically women became the standard-bearers in the church. Not only have they come to outnumber men in the pews, but they have also joined them as the laypreachers, cathecists and clergy. Not even the cunning colonial administrators could have foreseen this outcome.

Employing women teachers did not immediately lead to lower educational costs since the principle of equal pay for equal work for men and women was agreed on and implemented in elementary school teaching from 1900. However, over the long run it has, since teachers' salaries were increasingly regarded as a second income for a family. In the latter decades of the twentieth century this has led to increasing militancy among teachers seeking better remuneration.

In the conflict and competition between different social groups and vested interests, advantages gained during one period sometimes are subsequently reversed. Such was the case with the decisions of the Legislative Council and Department of Education to reduce the grant to Shortwood, reduce the teacher-training course to two instead of three years and to exclude academic subjects from the teachers' college curriculum. These decisions were later reversed by subsequent events or developments. Shortwood was expanded. The training period in colleges was restored to three years in 1911 (*Handbook of Jamaica* 1912: 330). Academic subjects were reintroduced into the teacher training curriculum in the 1920s and Mico men were allowed to sit the matriculation examinations of London University (Newman 1974: 12-14).

One of the few decisions of 1899 that was not reversed (nor was there subsequent protest or opposition) was the decision to shift the institutional provision for teacher training in favour of female instead of male teachers. For the period 1900 to 1956, the institutional provision remained the same, teacher recruitment and training stabilized around two-thirds female and one-third male. It became a permanent feature of the educational system. This would suggest that the same interplay of forces which produced the shift in the first place, continued to be operative for at least the next fifty-six years.

The state, at the end of the nineteenth century, having acquired control of the elementary school system shifted the channels of upward social mobility available to Blacks through education, in favour of females instead of males. This was done through the adoption of four measures:

(a) shifting the institutional provision so that there were three colleges training female teachers and only one college training male teachers. In addition, the enrolments of the female colleges were increased while that of the male college was decreased;

(b) offering larger schools additional posts on their establishments provided these posts were filled with female teachers;
(c) insisting that appointments to the post of headteacher be based on qualifications; and
(d) offering female teachers equal salaries with men, the only occupation at the time in which parity of pay for men and women obtained.

The question to be probed in this chapter is, what was the long term impact of this change on the structure of opportunities available to Blacks so that girls and not boys were favoured for upward social mobility through education?

IMPACT OF THE CHANGES MADE IN 1899

This section will examine the long term impact of the changes in the structure of opportunity on the participation and performance of black boys and girls in the education system in the first half of the twentieth century.

Participation of Boys and Girls in the School System

Bearing in mind the central importance of teachers' college education at that time to the upward mobility of Blacks, a shift in the gender composition of student admission and enrolment could be expected to have considerable impact on elementary schooling. This would be so because teachers' college admission would be one of the goals of successful completion of elementary schooling and therefore a major aspiration of elementary school students. The nature of the impact of the gender shift can be assessed by looking at enrolment in elementary schooling prior to and following the changes at the turn of the century.

Table 4.1 shows a general decline in elementary school enrolment between 1894 and 1920. Clearly the reforms which vocationalized elementary schooling and closed small schools had a negative effect on overall participation in elementary schooling. In 1894-95 elementary school enrolment displayed a male bias. By 1919-20 this had been reversed to a female bias. The shift in the gender bias in favour of girls in elementary school occurred in the second decade of the twentieth century, between 1910 and 1915 – about ten to fifteen years after the gender shift in teachers' college enrolment.

While elementary school enrolment expanded after 1920, the bias in enrolment in favour of girls remained in the elementary school system until 1965-70 when universal primary education was achieved in

Jamaica. In the postwar and post-Independence expansion of primary education, in the move to enrol all school age children, the gender bias in favour of girls was gradually eliminated.

Table 4.1 Elementary School Enrolment by Gender, 1894-1920

Year	Boys	%	Girls	%	Total
1894-1895	53,177	51.1	50,972	48.9	104,149
1899-1900	49,687	50.4	48,711	49.6	98,598
1904-1905	42,087	50.1	41,907	49.9	83,994
1909-1910	45,065	50.0	45,077	50.0	90,142
1914-1915	47,787	49.7	48,368	50.3	96,155
1919-1920	42,952	47.6	47,184	52.4	90,136
1925	56,853	48.2	61,021	51.8	117,874
1930	62,339	48.6	65,815	51.4	128,154
1935	71,854	48.6	76,060	51.4	147,914
1940	Not available – World War II				
1945	86,918	48.7	91,429	51.3	178,347
1950	96,704	48.4	103,655	51.6	199,832
1955	108,363	48.8	113.337	51.2	222,018
1959-1960	127,255	49.4	130,337	50.6	257,592
1963-1964	154,119	50.0	154,378	50.0	308,497
1968-1969	162,915	50.4	160,330	49.6	323,245
1989-1990	163,324	50.6	159,557	49.4	322,881

Source: Compiled from Blue Books and Ministry of Education statistics

The slightly higher enrolment of boys since the late 1960s has to be understood in the context of the demographic characteristics of Caribbean populations. The Jamaican population over the last 100 or more years, like most other populations in the Caribbean, has slightly more boys than girls in the age group from birth to fourteen years. This is because slightly more boys are born than girls. The slightly higher enrolment of boys (since practically every child of school age is enrolled in primary schools in Jamaica) represents parity between the genders in primary school enrolment. That slightly more boys are enrolled is but a manifestation of the demographic feature of the population and not a reemergence of a male bias.

What the data in Table 4.1 reveal is that for the fifty-year period 1914 to 1964, there were somewhat more girls than boys participating in primary schooling in Jamaica. This was the reverse of what obtained in the nineteenth century where more boys than girls were enrolled in elementary schooling. This observed shift in the participation of boys and girls in the elementary school system is confirmed when the Census

Table 4.2 Persons without Schooling in the Over-Ten Population 1943

Age	Male		Female		Total
	N	%	N	%	
10 - 14	12,545	62.2	7,630	37.8	20,175
15 - 19	11,145	61.1	7,109	38.9	18,254
20 - 24	11,797	55.1	9,618	44.8	21,415
25 - 29	12,627	54.4	10,590	45.6	23,217
30 - 34	13,169	55.3	10,645	44.7	23,812
35 - 39	12,394	54.5	10,267	45.5	22,661
40 - 44	11,383	54.6	9,470	45.4	20,853
45 - 49	8,204	53.0	7,289	47.0	15,493
50 - 54	6,733	49.5	6,881	50.5	13,614
55 - 59	4,423	47.2	4,943	52.8	9,366
60 - 64	4,447	45.0	5,444	55.0	9,891
65 - 69	2,368	32.3	4,952	67.7	7,320
70 & over	4,952	36.4	8,648	63.6	13,600

Source: Compiled from the census of 1943.

of 1943 is analysed in terms of the gender of persons over ten years old who never attended school.

Bearing in mind that the age of entry to elementary school was seven years up to 1964, then it can be seen from Table 4.2 that among the age groups eligible for entry before the turn of the century, that is, persons fifty years and older, it was more females than males who never attended school. These data show that among the older persons in the over-fifty age group in 1943, an increasing percentage of women never attended school.

For those eligible to enter school during the twentieth century, that is, persons under fifty years, the reverse was true: it was more males than females that never attended school. Indeed, of the persons under fifty years in 1943, the younger the persons the higher the percentage of boys who never attended school. The census data of 1943 corroborate the school enrolment data that after 1900 there was a significant decline in the participation of boys in elementary schooling.

Declining upward social mobility opportunities for black boys through the elementary school system seems to have led to decline in their participation in the school system. On the other hand, increased opportunities for upward social mobility through education seems to have encouraged the participation of girls in the elementary school system. The net result was that in the twentieth century, the pattern of participation of boys and girls in the elementary school system has been reversed, compared to the nineteenth century.

Performance of Boys and Girls in the School System

Literacy in the adult population is a general index of performance and achievement at the elementary level of the educational system. While the census data did not record literacy by gender before 1911, all the reports of educators and other observers in the nineteenth century concurred on the observation that more men were literate than women. This has been a worldwide pattern up to the present time. Table 4.3 shows literacy rates for men and women, over 15 years of age, as reported by the censuses between 1911 and 1943 and National Literacy Surveys between 1975 and 1987. In 1911 more Jamaican men were literate than women. In other words the pattern reported for the entire nineteenth century continued until the end of the first decade of the twentieth century. The difference in 1911 was slight, a mere 1.4 per cent. In all probability this difference was greater during the nineteenth century. By 1921, however, the situation had shifted to being slightly in favour of women. After that, the gap between adult male and female literacy became progressively wider in favour of women until it levelled off after 1975 to approximately ten percentage points. In 1911 the traditional pattern obtained in Jamaica: more men were literate than women. By 1921 the situation had been reversed: more women were literate than men. Since then the gap has widened.

Table 4.3 Literacy Levels of Jamaican Men and Women 1911-1987

Year	Men %	Women %	Overall %
1911	65.9	64.5	65.2
1921	65.1	67.3	66.3
1943	73.4	78.6	76.1
1975*	62.0	72.0	68.0
1981*	69.9	79.6	75.7
1987*	77.0	86.7	82.0

*The Functional Literacy Standard used since 1975 as against the Basic Standard used in 1911, 1921 and 1943.
Source: Compiled from censuses between 1911 and 1960 and National Literacy Surveys between 1975 and 1987.

Table 4.4 below shows that among Blacks and Coloureds there were distinctly more men who were illiterate than women. Among Chinese there were slightly more illiterate males than females. Among Whites, East Indians and Syrians more women were illiterate than men, reflecting the traditional pattern. The new pattern of more men being illiterate than women was observed among Blacks, Coloureds and Chinese. The female bias was most marked among the Blacks and Coloureds.

To interpret the data in Table 4.4 it is important to note the different types of schools that children of different races attended. Blacks and Browns were the major clients of the elementary schools although Browns living in urban centres and possessing the means sent their children to private schools. During this period significant numbers of Chinese children attended elementary schools. On the other hand, white and Syrian children typically attended private schools. In the case of Indians, up to the 1940s, the vast majority of children remained outside of the school system: they went to no school at all.

What Table 4.4 shows is that among Whites and Syrians who typically patronized private schools, and Indians who typically remained outside of the public school system, the traditional pattern of men being more literate than women prevailed. However, among those racial groups where the majority patronized the public elementary schools – Blacks, Coloureds and Chinese – more women were literate than men. Interestingly, after the Indians began to participate in the elementary school system the traditional pattern among this group was also reversed.

Table 4.4 Illiteracy Rates of Males and Females Seven Years of Age and Older 1943

Race/Colour	Males (%)	Females (%)
All races	28.4	23.0
Blacks	31.0	25.4
Coloureds	16.2	11.9
Chinese	14.6	13.0
Whites	3.4	4.1
Indians	45.3	51.9
Syrians	4.9	6.7

Source: Compiled from the census of 1943.

It seems reasonable to conclude that the long-term impact of the training and employment policies implemented between 1898 and 1900 was to shift the patterns of participation and performance among Blacks so that girls participated more and achieved better results in the school system than boys. The shift in the structure of opportunity in favour of black girls brought about corresponding shifts in both participation and performance in the school system. It would appear that the policies took about fifteen to twenty years to achieve their intended objective. By 1920 more girls were enrolled in elementary schools and more female students in teachers' colleges, and women had surpassed men in terms of literacy levels. These patterns remained unchanged for the first half of the twentieth century.

IMPACT OF POSTWAR POLICIES

This section will examine the impact, if any, of policies in the postwar period relative to the patterns and trends that had been established as a consequence of the policy directions set at the end of the nineteenth century. It will examine whether postwar policies have reversed or reinforced the patterns previously described.

The Gender Composition of the Elementary School Teaching Occupation

While the colonial administrators put in place policies to make elementary school teaching a female occupation, the question arises as to whether policies of the postwar and post-Independence era reversed those of the colonial era. Indeed, this has happened in several other areas of education.

In the postwar period there have been a number of reports or plans that have addressed educational policy. These include:

(a) The Kandel Report, 1943;
(b) The Ten-Year Plan of Development for Jamaica, 1947-1957;
(c) the National Plan, 1957-67;
(d) The Five-Year Independence Plan, 1963-1968;
(e) The UNESCO Report, 1964 (authored by Germanacos);
(f) The New Deal for Education, 1966;
(g) The Education Sector Survey, 1971;
(h) The Education Thrust of the Seventies, 1973; and
(i) Draft Five-Year Plan, 1978-83.
(k) The National Development Plan for Education, 1990-1995

All these plans and reports identify teachers and teacher training as important elements of educational and national development. All set targets for achieving a fully trained teaching force, having identified the backlog of untrained teachers in the primary school as an obstacle to the achievement of good quality primary education. Only the UNESCO Report of 1964 and the New Deal for Education of 1966, however, took note of the imbalance in the number of female teachers at the primary level. The UNESCO Report stated: "every effort should be made to introduce more men in the teaching profession" (*Education Planning*

Mission 1965: 45). The New Deal which drew heavily on the UNESCO Report in setting educational policies for the mid-1960s cautioned that "note must also be taken of the paucity of male students. This arises principally from the small numbers of boys who form the pool from which the various services and institutions can recruit. This situation can hardly be improved until such time as a pool of school leavers from high schools, technical high schools and the school of agriculture and similar institutions is ... increased" (*New Deal for Education* 1966: 84).

The substantial expansion of high schools, technical high schools, the School of Agriculture, and similar institutions did take place subsequent to the New Deal, financed mainly from loans from the World Bank, CIDA and USAID. However, the problem of the paucity of male students actually worsened, as their numbers deteriorated from the levels of the 1960s to even lower levels in the 1970s and 1980s. Further, there has been no special attempt to recruit male teachers.

The expansion of the educational system, and especially in teacher education, in the postwar period has been spectacular. By 1987, 95 per cent of the primary school teaching force had been trained. However, the bias in favour of females was not reversed; the opposite was true – it was made even greater (see Table 4.5).

Table 4.5 Primary and All-age School Teachers by Rank and Gender 1989-1990

	Male		Female		Total
Rank	N	%	N	%	
Principal	275	35.6	498	64.4	773
Vice-principal	20	5.7	328	94.3	348
Senior teacher	71	7.1	928	92.9	999
Trained teacher	543	8.2	6,040	91.8	6,583
Specialist	42	41.0	63	59.0	105
Pre-trained	214	16.9	1,053	83.1	1,267
Total	1,165	11.6	8,910	88.4	10,075

Source: Ministry of Education statistics, 1989-90

These data indicate that elementary school teaching is a predominantly female occupation (88.4 per cent of primary and all-age school teachers are female). Men, however, hold a disproportionate number of the top administrative positions as principals in the school system.

Although men comprise only 11.6 per cent of all teachers in primary and all-age schools, they hold 35.6 per cent of the posts of principal. Females, however, are overrepresented among vice-principals and senior teachers. They hold 94.3 and 92.9 per cent, respectively, of those posts. Among teachers without administrative responsibilities, women represent 91.8 per cent of the trained teachers, 59.0 per cent of the specialist teachers and 83.1 per cent of the pre-trained teachers.

Two points are worth noting from the above. First, while there are many other countries of the world in which women are the majority of the teachers, Jamaica is numbered among the few in which women also hold the majority of the posts of principal. For example, in the United States women are 77 per cent of the teachers but only 25 per cent of the principals. Tyack and Hansot (1982) make the point that women teach but men manage the schools. In terms of management, the Jamaican woman, often black, has made substantial progress in breaking into the management and administration of schools.

Secondly, while women are still underrepresented at the rank of principal, given their overrepresentation among vice-principals and senior teachers, one can reasonably expect that in the immediate future women will continue to narrow the gap between themselves and men at the rank of principal. A hundred years after the implementation of the policy to employ women as headteachers and teachers, the fulfilment of that policy objective is within sight. While women quickly overtook men as the teachers, overtaking them as principals has taken a longer time.

Much of the expansion of teacher education in the postwar and post-Independence periods was financed by external grants and loans from bilateral and multilateral donor agencies who, by their involvement, have become the latest accomplices in the process of the marginalization of the black man in Jamaica. None has identified his marginalization as an issue, let alone sought to address programmes or policies towards his integration into the mainstream of society.

The Integration of the Dual System of Education

As was stated previously, elementary schooling and teachers' colleges constituted one system of education, and preparatory schools and high schools another system. Because they served different social segments of the society and were administered separately, they constituted a dual system of education.

One of the major areas of change in education in the twentieth century has been in the attempts to integrate the dual system to form a single articulated system of schooling. While at first the pace was slow and the amount small, in the post-Independence period the pace has quickened and the magnitude has increased substantially. Over the years elementary school children have been gaining access to high schools and entry to teachers' colleges has been redefined in terms of successful completion of high schooling.

The major factor driving the integration of the school system has been postwar political reforms in which adult suffrage and representative government enfranchised the vast majority of Jamaicans who previously were excluded from government. The transfer of political power to the elected representatives of the people has occasioned corresponding reforms in the education system, of which the integration of the dual system is but one outcome.

Significant milestones in the integration process have been the common entrance and free place reforms of 1957 which determined that entry to high schooling would be based on merit; the phasing out of the pupil-teacher system and its examinations in the 1960s; and the reform of teacher education in 1981, which prescribed access to teacher education in terms of GCE/CXC passes and required the same standards as applied to entry to sixth form. The end result of these reforms is that primary school students now seek entry to high schools as their major goal; and teaching, through preparation in teachers' college, is one of the career options open to high school leavers.

Apart from the integration of the school system, the transfer of political power has occasioned significant expansion of opportunities at all levels of the school system. Primary education has become universal and secondary education has achieved mass status in that more than 60 per cent of the twelve to seventeen age cohort receive some form of secondary education for five years. The coveted high school education has also undergone dramatic expansion. From an enrolment of just over 4,000 pupils in 1943, high school enrolment exceeded 55,000 in 1985.

Table 4.6 School Background of Students Entering High Schools 1942-1982

	Primary school	Preparatory school
1942	45.0	55.0
1961	47.0	53.0
1965	70.0	30.0
1970	66.7	33.3
1975	74.4	25.6
1980	85.8	14.2
1985	84.0	16.0
1990	81.5	18.5

Source: Department of Education and Ministry of Education statistics.

The data from Table 4.6 suggest that in the period in which high schooling was expanded significantly, primary school students gained an increasing proportion of the places that were created, although over the decade of the 1980s preparatory students seemed to have improved their share. In 1990 preparatory schools accounted for just about 7 per cent of total enrolment of the six to twelve age group in schools while primary schools account for 93 per cent of total enrolment. The data from Table 4.6 indicate that primary school students still have some more to go in being truly representative in high schools, and that preparatory school students still enjoy some advantage in access to high schooling. However, in relation to the disparity that existed in the 1940s, primary school students have made substantial progress in gaining access to high schooling.

Notwithstanding these efforts and the successes achieved, elementary education is still terminal for a significant proportion of students. Forty per cent of school-age children are forced to terminate their education at age fifteen, the school leaving age of the all-age, or elementary, school. Further access to the prestigious high schools has only been increased to 20 per cent of the age cohort over the decade of the 1980s. For most of the period of Independence it was restricted to only 10 per cent.

The question that must be addressed is whether the replacement of the teachers' college by the high school as the immediate channel of upward mobility available to Blacks has made any difference to the gender patterns of participation and performance previously described in this chapter. This leads to another question, that of whether the gender structure of opportunity available through high schooling is any different from that which obtained through teachers' colleges during the first half of the twentieth century.

Miller (1990) showed that when Blacks gained access to high schooling in the postwar period, the same gender patterns of opportunity which obtained at the end of the nineteenth century, repeated themselves. Table 4.7 compares the forty-six traditional high schools in Jamaica on the basis of the gender of students in high schools established prior to 1940 and those added to the public system after 1940.

Table 4.7 High Schools by Gender: Before and After 1940

	NUMBER AND TYPE OF SCHOOL			
Period	**Boys**	**Girls**	**Coed.**	**Total**
Established before 1940	7	9	6	22
Established after 1940	–	6	18	24
Total	7	15	24	46

Source: Miller (1990)

This table also shows that there was close to a balance between the genders among high schools established before 1940. There were seven boys' schools, nine girls' schools and six coeducational schools. While girls' schools had a slight edge, they were generally the smaller schools; hence the slight bias in number of schools could be offset by size. Among the schools incorporated into the public system in the postwar period there has been a clear bias in favour of girls. While the policy direction has been generally towards coeducation in that eighteen of the twenty-four schools added to the system were coeducational, it is also true that six girls' schools were added and not a single boys' school. This has meant that in the expanded high school system that has been created in the postwar period there has been more than twice the number of girls' schools compared to boys' schools, although coeducational schools have become the most common type of high school (see Table 4.8).

Table 4.8 Enrolment by Gender of Schools Established Before and After 1940

	Enrolment 1984-85				
	Boys		Girls		Total
Schools by period	*N*	%	*N*	%	
Estab. before 1940	12,271	46.0	13,948	54.0	26,219
Estab. after 1940	10,154	35.2	18,713	64.8	28,867
Total	22,425	40.4	32,661	59.6	55,086

Source: Miller (1990)

This table shows that the enrolment of schools that were established before 1940 revealed a bias in favour of females, which was consistent with the slight bias in the gender structure of those schools. On the other hand, schools established after 1940 showed a considerable bias in favour of girls. This also was consistent with the gender structure of these institutions. In other words, the clear enrolment bias favouring girls was entirely consistent with the gender biases of the institutional structure. The institutional structure provided more high school places for girls; hence, there were more girls than boys enrolled in high schools.

Miller (1990) examined the gender differences in relation to social class and found that these differences are not evenly distributed across the different classes. Table 4.9 shows the social class differences of boys and girls, in 1982, entering the twenty-six high schools included in Miller's sample. The data show that whereas 42.1 per cent of the students entering high schools in 1982 were boys and 57.9 per cent were girls, this gender difference in access to high schooling was not evenly distributed across all social classes. Among the upper-class students

Table 4.9 Social Class by Gender: Students Entering High School in 1982

	Boys		Girls		Total
Social Class	*N*	%	*N*	%	
Upper	27	50.0	27	50.0	54
Traditional Middle	768	44.0	979	56.0	1,747
Emerging Middle	719	40.5	1,057	59.5	1,776
Lower	271	40.7	395	59.3	666
Total	1,785	42.1	2,458	57.9	4,243

Source: Adapted from Miller (1990)

there was parity: an equal number of boys and girls gained access to high schools. However, as the social ladder was descended the differences between the proportion of boys and girls widened. Among traditional middle-class students there was a noticeable bias in favour of girls, while among emerging middle and lower-class students there was a distinct bias in favour of girls. Approximately 60 per cent of the children from the emerging middle and lower classes entering high schools were female.

It should be noted that Manley (1963) studying students entering high schools in 1959 found there were gender differences in the primary and preparatory school students gaining access to high schools. While 52 per cent of the preparatory school students were boys and 48 per cent girls, in the case of the primary school students it was 39 per cent boys and 61 per cent girls. By the early 1970s this gender difference between primary and preparatory students had disappeared. Both types of schools now send more girls than boys to high school.

Gordon (1991) examined access to high schooling in relationship to race, class, gender and cohort. In investigating the influence of gender, Gordon looked at cohorts gaining access to high schooling between 1936 and 1975. Gordon found that in the higher social classes males continued to have an advantage over females independent of race. However, in the middle classes there appeared to be some weakening of the advantage in the more recent cohorts. Among the working class, Gordon found that black girls had an advantage over black boys in gaining access to high schooling, and this advantage again seems to be more marked in the more recent cohorts.

The clear inference to be drawn from these data and studies is that high schooling in the postwar period has come to manifest the same gender bias in the structure of educational opportunities that emerged in teacher education at the turn of the twentieth century. The replacement of teacher college education by high schooling as the most immediate route of upward social mobility for Blacks has therefore made no difference to the patterns of participation of Blacks in the school system that had emerged over the first half of this century.

Miller (1992), in his survey of the performance of primary students in 1989 in the Grade Six achievement tests of the National Assessment Programme (NAP), found that gender was a factor in the performance of students in all subjects. Girls performed better than boys in reading, language and mathematics while boys performed better than girls in science and social studies. In the Common Entrance examinations, girls performed better than boys in all subjects. Interestingly, the subjects that boys performed best in, science and social studies, are not included in the Common Entrance examinations. As far as performance is concerned, at the end of primary schooling girls continue to hold a distinct advantage over boys in Jamaica. The integration of elementary and high schooling has certainly made no difference to the gender patterns of performance previously described.

The articulation of elementary schooling with high schooling has apparently widened the impact of the gender patterns, given the larger size of the high school system. By offering significantly more opportunities, high schooling seems to have had an even more pervasive effect than teachers' college education. Further, by the 1950s the primary school system had already been biased in participation and performance in favour of girls; hence, articulation with the high school system that has institutionalized a feminine bias has only perpetuated and deepened the already established bias in primary schooling.

As Miller (1990) pointed out, when access to high schooling was democratized to allow access to Blacks in significant numbers, the slight gender bias that had emerged by the late 1930s was deepened by policies which allowed girls' and coeducational schools to be added to the system without any corresponding addition of boys' schools. What this meant was that by the 1950s both high schooling and teachers' colleges, the two main avenues of upward social mobility, were decidedly biased in favour of access to girls.

Enrolment in secondary schools and of Jamaicans at the University of the West Indies (UWI) is shown in Tables 4.10, 4.11 and 4.12.

Table 4.10 shows types of secondary level education and relative rank in terms of social prestige as judged by the potential of the various levels to provide upward social mobility. The mode of access to these different types of schools is one indicator of their social rank. Entry to the traditional high school is through the Common Entrance examination. Entry to the comprehensive high school is mixed between

Table 4.10 Enrolment in Secondary Schools by Gender 1989-90

	Male		Female		Total
Type of school and ranking	*N*	%	*N*	%	
1. Traditional high	28,789	42.0	39,776	58.0	68,565
2. Comprehensive high	3,660	43.3	4,801	56.7	8,461
3. Technical high	6,634	47.4	7,367	52.6	14,001
4. Vocational high	438	48.0	474	52.0	912
5. All-age (Grades 7-9)	30,850	51.6	28,911	48.4	59,761
6. New secondary	38,693	52.3	35,315	47.7	74,008
Total	109,064	48.3	116,644	51.7	225,708

Source: Ministry of Education statistics, 1989-90.

selection through the Common Entrance examinations and automatic promotion from neighbouring primary schools. Entrance to the technical high school is through the Technical Entrance examination sat one year after the Common Entrance; while entry to the vocational school is through the Grade Nine Achievement test. Entry to the all-age school is by automatic promotion from Grade Six; however, students sit the Grade Nine Achievement test and have some opportunity to enter one of the types of high school whose entry depends upon selection. Entry to the new secondary school is non-selective and is related to automatic promotion from neighbouring primary schools.

Table 4.10 shows that enrolment in the traditional high and comprehensive high schools is distinctly biased towards females. A slight female bias is also observed with the respect to technical and vocational high school enrolment. However, with respect to the all-age and new secondary schools which offer very little prospect of upward social mobility, the enrolment is slightly male biased.

Table 4.10 also shows that more girls than boys are enrolled in all types of secondary schools. Given the fact that between the ages of twelve and eighteen there is virtual parity between the sexes in the population, the bias in secondary school enrolment would suggest a greater drop-out rate of boys than girls, among students going beyond primary schooling.

Table 4.11 shows the total number of Jamaicans enrolled at the UWI in 1990-91: full-time and part-time, and in all programmes. It shows that Jamaican women significantly outnumbered men 3,613 to 2,244 (61.7 per cent compared to 38.3 per cent). This higher proportion of women was reflected at all levels: certificate, diploma, first degree and higher degree. Indeed, the gender gap was widest at the higher degree level: 63.4 per cent women compared to 36.6 per cent men.

Table 4.11 Jamaican Students Enrolled at UWI 1990-91

Programme	Male N	Male %	Female N	Female %	Total
Certificate	70	26.1	198	74.9	268
Diploma	112	44.6	139	55.4	251
First Degree	1,771	39.0	2,772	61.0	4,543
Higher Degree	291	36.6	504	63.4	795
Total	2,244	38.3	3,613	61.7	5,857

Source: The University of the West Indies statistics, 1990/91.

Table 4.12 shows that Engineering was the only Faculty in which Jamaican men had a decided advantage over Jamaican women. In Agriculture men enjoyed a slight advantage, while in Natural Sciences the scales were almost even. In Medicine and all the other Faculties women held a distinct advantage.

When the data in Tables 4.10, 4.11 and 4.12 are taken together it seems reasonable to conclude that postwar policies in education have widened the gender gap in education in Jamaica in favour of women. Far from reversing patterns of the colonial era, the post-Independence policy has enhanced the gender patterns created in the first half of the twentieth century.

Table 4.12 First Degree Full-Time Jamaican Students Enrolled at UWI by Faculty and Gender 1990-91

Faculty	Male N	Male %	Female N	Female %	Total
Arts & General Studies	170	22.4	590	77.6	760
Education	33	24.3	103	75.7	136
Law	29	26.1	82	73.9	111
Social Sciences	345	37.7	569	62.3	914
Agriculture	13	52.0	12	48.0	25
Engineering	150	91.5	14	8.5	164
Medicine	124	44.6	154	55.4	278
Natural Sciences	547	50.9	527	49.1	1074
Total	1,411	40.8	2,051	59.2	3,462

Source: The University of the West Indies statistics 1990/91.

SOCIALIZATION PATTERNS OF HOME AND SCHOOL

The most pervasive impact of the gender bias in the structure of opportunity has been its reversal of socialization patterns in the home and school. Any analysis, therefore, could not be complete without reference to this aspect.

Parents doing their own private rate of return analyses invest more in their children who are mostly likely to succeed. This is particularly so among parents with very limited resources. Where the structure of opportunities gives those opportunities mainly to boys, the socialization patterns of the home are likely to favour sons. Where the reverse is true then they are more likely to favour daughters.

Likewise, elementary school teachers doing similar analyses invest more in the students most likely to succeed, particularly where the teachers' reputations depend upon examination results. If male students are most likely to succeed, efforts will be concentrated on boys. If girls are most likely to succeed, then teachers will invest more in the female students rather than their male counterparts. The socialization pattern of the school is likely to be biased in favour of the gender most likely to succeed in the particular society.

The data in this chapter seem to suggest that after the structure of mobility opportunities open to Blacks was shifted in favour of females instead of males, this led to a reversal of the socializing patterns of black homes and the schools serving them. Within ten to fifteen years after the gender shift in the structure of opportunities, participation and performance began to reveal gender biases consistent with the bias in opportunities.

The theory of place maintains that the basic motivation in society is for individuals to gain and retain central places. Hence, access to those institutions of the educational system which offer greater prospects for its members to gain or retain central places will have an inspirational effect on achievement on the lower levels of the system related to them.

Educational systems are hierarchically organized. So, too, is knowledge in the several disciplines. From a functionalist perspective mastery at the lower levels of the educational system is crucial to successful performance at the upper levels. The basic assumption is that mastery at the lower level is prerequisite to learning at the upper levels, since complex principles taught at the upper levels are composed of combinations of basic concepts learned at the lower levels. One truism that has resulted from this argument is that sound primary education is an absolute essential for good secondary education.

From the perspective of the theory of place the impact between levels of the educational system is not unidirectional, from lower to upper, but reciprocal. That is, the upper levels also have an impact on learning and achievement at the lower levels. This reciprocal relationship between upper and lower levels is predicated on the assumption that the structure of the educational system is not only related to the structure of knowledge, but also to the place structure of the society and the motivation of individuals and groups in society to improve their places in society. Access to those sections of the upper levels of the educational system which give maximum facility for upward social mobility will have a significant impact on achievement at the lower levels of the educational system, particularly among those individuals and groups which use, or are restricted to use, education as their major avenue of social mobility.

The assertion here is that while the upper sections of the educational system that offer upward social mobility may be relatively small compared to the rest of the system, their impact is pervasive because they influence the striving of much larger numbers of persons than those who actually gain entry. The impact of these sections of the educational system belies their size. While they are restricted in size, their effect on learning, achievement and participation is pervasive. In addition, the impact of the upper levels is quite strong. The strength of the upper sections resides in the intensity of the striving of those who are marginalized to improve their place in society through the educational system. Accordingly, manipulation of access to the upper levels of the educational system can have profound effects on participation and achievement in the educational system, including changing traditional relationships.

The gender patterns set in the first half of the twentieth century have not been reversed in the latter half of the century. Indeed, all the evidence points to the fact that they have been exaggerated in the second half of the century. Both Gordon (1987) and Miller (1990) have found that in the postwar period black girls have experienced more upward social mobility than black boys. The latter are much more likely to inherit their parents' socioeconomic status than are their sisters. While the sons are more likely to be peasant/agricultural labourers, their sisters, with superior educational achievements and credentials, are more likely to join the urban drift and find employment in white-collar occupations.

The end result is that spread of matrifocal forms in black families as their women take the lead in education, jobs and income. Traditional gender roles and relationships have been reversed and radically altered. Also related to this is the growing alienation of young black men from mainstream society and their congregation in violent and deviant subculture and cults. Probably the most ironic aspect of these changes is that Blacks have internalized the patterns imposed and accepted responsibility for the outcomes.

5

Conclusion and Implications

FEMINIZATION OF TEACHING

The feminization of the teaching profession has been the subject of study in several countries. A common North American explanation is that the gender composition of elementary school teaching shifted from being male to female principally as a result of market forces (Bryans 1974; Tyack and Stober 1981). A strong demand for teachers, coupled with a growing supply of literate young women created by elementary schooling, led to the feminization of teaching in circumstances where men left teaching for more lucrative jobs in industry, or parsimonious school boards employed women because they could be paid less.

This explanation of the feminization of teaching could probably hold for private school teachers in Jamaica, if one understands that these schools have largely catered to children of the higher socioeconomic groups in the society and as such have been staffed largely by the women of these social groups. In other words, it is women's marginalization in the groups holding power and position in society that accounts for their predominance in the teaching occupation in the private sector.

The history of the feminization of public elementary school teaching in Jamaica, however, provides no evidence that market forces played any role whatsoever. While there was always strong demand for teachers, and while elementary school teaching became a mainly black male occupation by 1850, there is no empirical evidence that black men in the twentieth century were moving to more lucrative occupations and therefore were replaced by a growing pool of literate black women. Throughout the hundred-year period between 1850 and 1950, the prospects for black men gaining access to lucrative and white-collar occupations were extremely limited. Further, substantial improvement in the literacy rate among black women, seemed to have been a consequence and not a cause of their gaining access to the elementary school teaching occupation.

Neither is there any evidence to suggest that women were initially employed as teachers because they could be paid less than men. On the contrary, the pay policy in elementary school teaching in Jamaica has always been to pay women the same salaries as men. While such pay differentials existed among secondary school teachers, and while some advocated the same policy for elementary school teachers, such a policy was never implemented or practised in the elementary school system in Jamaica.

The explanation for the feminization of public elementary school teaching in Jamaica is not to be found in functional factors related to supply and demand and the operation of the market. Rather, it is to be found in the place theory's assertions about the outcomes of the contest between centrals and marginals for place in society, and the location and control of the occupation of elementary school teaching in that contest.

FINDINGS IN RELATIONS TO THE HYPOTHESES

In chapter 2 four hypotheses were derived and postulated (see page 38). The findings from the study with respect to each hypothesis need to be discussed in turn.

Hypothesis 1

> Given the segmentation in the education queue and the separate control of the dual system of education by the groups they serve, it can be expected that Blacks and their allies would attempt to make the denominational system a parallel and equal schooling to the private/trust system, while the white and brown upper and middle-status groups would seek to make the denominational school system subordinate and inferior to the private/trust school system.

The dual system of education was officially abolished in 1950. For the century or more that it existed there was perennial conflict between the different social segments with respect to the status and position of the two systems. While the Blacks and their allies attempted to make the elementary school and the teachers' college the parallel and equal of the preparatory and the high school, the white and brown élite invariably sought to make the former the inferior of the latter.

Nowhere was the conflict more evident than with respect to the curriculum to be taught in the two sets of institutions. It was generally accepted that preparatory and high school education should be general and liberal with a bias towards the classics. From the inauguration of the elementary/teachers' college system there was divergence on the curriculum to be taught. For the Blacks and their allies the denominational system should follow the same curriculum as the endowed system. Hence, for as long as they had control of the denominational system the curriculum was general and liberal with a bias towards the classics.

The planter controlled state insisted that the curriculum of the mass system should be centred around literacy, numeracy and vocational skills. For the entire period of denominational control of elementary education, the state repeatedly failed in its efforts to reform the system in that direction. However, within a decade of gaining control of the elementary/teachers' college system, the state gutted the elementary and teachers' college curriculum of the classics, humanities and sciences and imposed a curriculum stressing literacy, numeracy, agriculture, manual training and domestic economy. At the very same time the state strengthened the high schools' capacity to offer a sound liberal education.

The history of the dual system of education in Jamaica is entirely consistent with Hypothesis 1. While Blacks and their allies sought to maximize upward social mobility through the elementary school/teachers' college system, the ruling élite sought to minimize such prospects. The extent to which these intentions could be openly and manifestly pursued depended largely on which group controlled the system. Shifts in control resulted in corresponding shifts in focus and content. The historical evidence entirely supports Hypothesis 1.

Hypothesis 2

> Where Blacks gain and retain control over the denominational school system, upward social mobility opportunities would be biased in favour of males. That is, opportunities to advance from elementary schools to teachers' colleges would be biased in favour of black males served by the denominational system.

Blacks gained effective control of the denominational system following the phasing out of the Negro Education Grant in 1845. They retained control until 1892 when the state assumed responsibility for elementary education and offered it free to children of school age. All the available empirical data, as well as the documented accounts of the period testify to the fact that during the period between 1845 and 1892 it was black males that enjoyed the vast majority of the limited upward social mobility opportunities that Blacks gained. The data and the documents all confirm Hypothesis 2.

The evidence is unequivocal and clear that for as long as Blacks controlled access to education, they followed the patriarchal tradition of favoring males for social advancement in the public sphere. The socializing pattern of the home and school and the prevailing mentality were consistent and supportive of this pattern.

Hypothesis 3

> Where control of the denominational system falls into the hands of the ruling élite through the state machinery, upward social mobility through education would be shifted in favour of black females.

From 1879 the planter élite openly advocated the replacing of black males by black females as elementary school teachers. Prior to 1892, the crown colony administrators, however, only made modest concessions to this demand. They closed the government training college for male teachers after they had established a government training college for female teachers. Seven years after the state took control of the elementary school system, both the colonial administrators and the church leadership, for their own conflicting and concealed reasons, capitulated to the policy openly advocated by the planter élite. Both the teacher training and employment policies were deliberately biased towards women teachers. The end result was that by the second decade of the twentieth century the gender composition of elementary school teaching shifted in favour of females. The empirical evidence concerning the shift from male to female teachers in Jamaica is consistent with Hypothesis 3.

Hypothesis 4

> Attempts to integrate the society and the school systems would lead to further bias in favour of black females gaining access to educational opportunities leading to upward social mobility.

The postwar period was characterized by sustained attempts to integrate the society through democratizing access to all institutions. In education, these attempts focused on access to high schooling and access to tertiary education. During this period the gender bias in elementary school teaching widened. In 1951 men were 32.0 per cent of the teachers being trained; by 1985 they had declined to 10.6 per cent of the teachers being prepared to teach in primary schools. In 1951 men were 20.9 per cent of the elementary school teachers; however, by 1990 they had declined to 11.6 per cent of the total number of primary school teachers. The data concerning the widening gender bias in elementary school teaching during the postwar period support Hypothesis 4.

Place in the Jamaican Society

The confirmation of the four hypotheses, derived from the place theory as applied to the Jamaican society, should permit some observations about place in the Jamaican society and, in the process, about place theory itself.

Changes in the Operational Absolutes

Chapter 2 identified race, class, gender, and age as the operational absolutes on which the Jamaican society was organized immediately following Emancipation. From the case study that followed, it is clear that changes have occurred among the operational absolutes. These changes can be listed briefly as follows:

(a) Class and race have shifted position in the hierarchy of operational absolutes. Class is now the principal absolute, while race/colour operates within class. This could be interpreted to indicate the declining significance of race. The deeper significance, however, relates to the shifting relationship between ascriptive and achievement categories in determining the place structure, that is, inequality in society. The Jamaican society organized on the basis of race, class, gender, and age, was dominated by ascriptive criteria but permitted achievement within the limits of those ascriptions. The Jamaican society so organized, elevates achievement as the principal criterion, but then biases and distorts it on the basis of ascriptions.

The latter is harder and more difficult to justify and legitimize. For example, the elevation of class as the premier criterion has made education credentials much more important as one of the measures in allocating place in society. However, it is very difficult to justify and legitimize race, gender, and age as qualifiers of access to the type of education that would lead to the acquisition of the desired education credentials. Why should persons of a particular race, gender, or age have greater access to schooling that leads to the coveted credentials, if individual achievement is the principal criterion?

(b) The shift in the relative relationship between race and class as operational absolutes, has resulted in greater racial integration at all levels of the society, but especially among the centrals. Hence, Blacks, Browns, Whites, Indians, Chinese and Lebanese/Syrians are all numbered among the centrals in the society. This, however, has not meant that the centrals now behave significantly differently towards marginals as some had predicted or anticipated. This explains, for example, why some patterns and relationships, noted in the society when it was almost segregated along racial lines, still persist and are even exaggerated in this phase of great racial integration.

(c) Gender and age roles and relationships, as traditionally defined in the Jamaican society, have been seriously compromised. Skipping significant number of young women in the place queue has compromised both age and gender as operational absolutes. Their advancement above their mothers and fathers has compromised age, because younger generations have exceeded those that bore them. Young people have therefore performed roles that were previously restricted to older people. Likewise, by advancing some women over the brothers, fathers, and husbands, gender roles and relationships, as traditionally defined, have been compromised.

(d) From the foregoing it can be seen that both configuration of the operational absolutes and individual operational absolutes are seriously flawed and compromised. The result is a crisis of the basis on which the Jamaican society is organized. The old bases of accounting for and justifying inequality are obviously flawed and increasingly unacceptable, while new bases for restructuring the society are not widely accepted or agreed.

The old ideology of superiority/inferiority in relation to race, gender, and age has been largely discredited, as well as seriously compromised. At the same time the ideology of a meritocracy based on personal competence and individual achievement has not taken root because of the undertones of race, gender, and seniority which are evident in most institutions. The result is uncertainty and confusion of roles, relationships, value systems, and attitudes. Further, the future direction of the society in resolving the crisis is neither clear nor assured.

Changes in the Place Queue in Education

Using the work of Gordon (1987, 1991) and Miller (1990) it is possible to construct the place queue for education in contemporary Jamaican society. Table 5.1 below shows a comparison of the contemporary queue with that previously described at the time of Emancipation. The following should be observed from the comparisons:

Table 5.1 Place Queue in Education Compared, 1837 and 1990s

Queue in 1837	Queue in the 1990s
Segment A	
1. White upper-class male	1. Upper-class light-skinned male
2. Brown upper-class male	2. Upper-class dark-skinned male
3. White middle-class male	3. Middle-class light skinned male
4. White lower-class male	4. Upper-class light-skinned female
Brown middle-class male	Middle-class light-skinned female
Black upper-class male	5. Upper-class dark-skinned female
5. White middle-class female	6. Middle-class dark-skinned male
Brown middle-class female	7. Middle-class dark-skinned female
6. Brown middle-class female	8. Lower-class light-skinned female
Black upper-class female	9. Lower-class dark-skinned female
7. White upper-class female	10. Lower-class light-skinned male
----------------	11. Lower-class dark-skinned male
Segment B	
8. Black middle-class male	
Brown lower-class male	
9. Black lower-class male	
Black middle-class female	
10. White lower-class female	
Brown lower-class female	
Black lower-class female	

(a) The place queue in education is no longer segregated. On the contrary, it is integrated. This is so by virtue of the fact that all segments of the society currently have access to and participate in the same educational institutions. While that access and participation are not exploited to the same degree by all segments, no segment or group is excluded from any level or institution.

(b) Class in the 1990s is the premier criterion, and the distinction between white and brown has collapsed into "light-skinned", a categorization which is able to accommodate Chinese and Lebanese/Syrians. "Dark-skinned" is the modern representation of black.

(c) The top positions in the queue are still dominated by men. The biggest change in the top positions is that upper class dark-skinned men have moved up in the queue and are now rivalling or challenging their light-skinned peers. However, light-skinned men still occupy the top position.

(d) The middle positions in the queue are predominantly held by females with the notable exception of middle-class dark-skinned men.
(e) Lower-class women's position in the queue is reversed relative to lower-class men.
(f) Lower-class men now occupy the bottom positions in the queue and dark-skinned men the lowest position. This position of lower-class men means that men's position in the queue is highly polarized. Upper-class men occupy the top positions, while lower-class men occupy the bottom positions.
(g) While the education queue of 1837 could be said to represent colour/class patriarchy, patriarchal principles of societal organization are seriously compromised in the contemporary queue. This is particularly so among lower-class men. It is the lower-class women who are preferred for social advancement, through education, over the lower-class men.

The Separation in Time of Cause and Effect

When the Jamaican case study of gender changes is examined in its entirety, one of the striking observations is the length of the separation in time between cause and effect. The Morant Bay Rebellion was a momentous event in the history of Jamaica and indeed of the Caribbean. In moving to address the issues over which black men had taken up arms, the crown colony administration had implemented measures which gave promise of social advancement for Blacks. Given the patriarchal traditions that existed among Blacks, such advancement would go to black men.

The planter élite, the historical societal adversaries, while not opposing the notion that opportunities for social advancement should be given to Blacks, began to advocate that that advancement, available to Blacks through teacher training and elementary school teaching, should go to black women. This notion began to be voiced in the 1870s. It took over twenty years before this became official policy and a further twenty years before that policy began to produce the desired effect in elementary education. Further, it took another fifty years before this pattern became pervasive in the society. In other words, it took nearly a century before the societal patterns advocated in the 1870s became a reality. None of the early conceptualizers of this notion lived to see even its accomplishments within the education system.

This long separation in time between cause and effect in social phenomena obscures the relationship since it permits of so many intervening variables and casts doubt on causal connections with past policies, programmes, and events, probably long forgotten. The caution to social scientists and educators is to avoid the mistake of interpreting education, gender, and other social phenomena outside of a historical context. Without a historical sequence, monumental mistakes could be made in interpreting social change.

Marginality in Place Theory

In place theory, marginality is not a permanent, hopeless or terminal condition. Rather, it is one of the unequal positions in society. Like anything else, marginality could be positive or negative. This conceptualization of marginality is amply represented by reference to the position of young black lower-class women in the Jamaican case study. In 1837, young black lower-class women were the most marginalized members of the Jamaican society. They were marginalized on the basis of being black, of being young, of being lower class and of being female.

The position of the young black lower-class female has not remained unchanged over the years since 1837. In the context of contest for position in society between Blacks and other groups, the marginality of young black lower-class females made them attractive as the beneficiaries of sponsored mobility. This has created the circumstances through which black females could begin to break out of women's historical marginality in society. Accordingly, many young black females have begun to benefit from the release of marginal energy: the motive and momentum derived from the prospect of overcoming marginality. The prospect and possibility of upward mobility through legitimate means have inspired many young black women to seek to achieve positions that hitherto were denied their mothers and grandmothers, and women generally.

The instance of young black lower-class females is used to illustrate the point that marginality in society can have positive connotations where there are prospects of movement away from the marginal condition. What is released is marginal energy: motive and momentum to strive to achieve. According to place theory this is the dynamic in society: the real prospect of moving from a marginal to a more central position in society.

By the same logic, marginality can have negative connotations where there is the real possibility of movement from a more central to a more marginal position. The movement of young black men down the place queue is one such example. By not seeing any real prospect of legitimate means of moving away from the marginal position, but rather of becoming even more marginalized, young black lower-class males can be seen to manifest many of the negative aspects of marginality.

IMPLICATIONS

The foregoing discussion has demonstrated that the marginalization of the black man in the Jamaican educational system has been the result of a complex interaction of social, economic, and political factors operating in the interrelationships between different ethnic groups in the Jamaican society, coupled with shifts in the balance of advantage between one group or another during different periods of Jamaican history. The evidence of the social, economic, and political factors which have shaped the development of teacher education and, consequently, teacher supply and employment is totally consistent with place theory.

Primary school teaching and teacher education shifted from being male dominated to being female dominated as a result of the intention of those holding central positions in the society to restrict black men to occupations related to agricultural and industrial labour; to stifle the possible emergence of militant black educated men who could possibly overthrow the power structure; to loosen the hold of the church on the education system; and to limit the upward social mobility of black men in the society.

In a real sense the black woman was deliberately used against the black man. In essence the logic seems to have been that if social advantage must be conceded to Blacks through teacher education and elementary school teaching, then allow black women such advancement instead of black men.

In this regard it is important to note that bias related to race/colour and gender have been institutionalized in the Jamaican educational system. It is important to recognize that these race/colour and gender biases are institutional and not personal or individual discrimination. No one is actively discriminating or personally keeping black individuals from access to all levels of educational opportunity. However, the structure of the system is such that there are innumerable obstacles in the way of those who attend public primary schools, teacher colleges and other institutions that have catered mainly to the black population. Despite repeated attempts to reform and integrate the education system, overtones of the dual system still persist. High schooling is still not fully integrated with primary schools. Rather, primary schooling leads to unimpeded promotion to types of secondary schooling which offer limited prospects of upward social mobility.

The gender biases are also institutionalized but, in addition, they are convoluted. They are nested in overlays of contradiction. They give the impression of liberating women but at the same time consign them to the less privileged and less powerful positions in society. The class ceiling is very much in evidence although it would appear that advantages are being given to women. While allowed greater access to upward mobility, this is to a point beyond which women find it most difficult to proceed. Thus women are often frustrated by not being rewarded with top positions commensurate with their ability and experience.

Both institutional racism and convoluted sexism are servants of the same purpose – the retention of power, wealth, and status by men of the ruling minorities. They are instruments of marginalization.

The most interesting aspect of the marginalization process in Jamaica is that persons of all ethnic groups and both sexes participate in marginalizing themselves and others without seeming to be aware of what they are actually doing. Marginality has become such an integral part of socialization and social intercourse that it has become almost habitual, devoid of consciousness. Blacks, Browns, Whites, Jews, Lebanese, East Indians and Chinese are implicated in the institutionalized racial patterns. Women and men are implicated in marginalizing themselves and each other; yet all would plead innocence to the charge with passion and sincerity. In such circumstances, the patterns perpetuate themselves without being noticed.

There are a number of implications which need to be discussed, even if only briefly.

Implications for Education Policies

The weight of evidence in this study seems to suggest that post-Independence educational policies have not taken sufficient account of developments in the crown colony period 1865-1944. They have also ignored the sociological meaning and impact of these developments. These historical and sociological shortcomings of post-Independence policy making has meant that it has not fundamentally altered important patterns in the society. Indeed, it may have made matters worse.

For example, the matter of achieving a better balance of male and female teachers in the school system is now more difficult to achieve than in the 1960s. This is an important consideration for the socialization of both boys and girls in a society in which effective male influence is often absent from the home.

It is also apparent that patterns in the society and in the school system came about by deliberate actions in the past and can also be effectively changed by similarly deliberate actions. Certainly, quantitative increases cannot meaningfully address the qualitative changes that are required. At the same time, there seems to be no emerging consensus about the type of society or civilization that the schools should be seeking to create. The old bases of society are compromised, but how the society should be reorganized is still unclear. Schooling in Jamaica seems to be operating without an overall societal mission.

Some aspects of future policy making seem clear. It would appear that the policy of coeducation needs re-examination, certainly within secondary and tertiary education. This is not to say that boys and girls, men and women should not be educated together. The question is whether or not an equal number of places should not be allocated to each gender in each institution and the best candidates of each gender selected for the number of places available for each gender. This would eliminate competition for places between men and women.

Also, there is justification for exposing all students to all areas of the curriculum without reference to the gender of the students. Hence girls should be exposed to all areas of science and technology and boys to home economics and foreign languages. Again, some consideration should be given to teaching boys and girls separately in such subjects, especially where there is evidence of gender biases in relation to access and performance in those subjects. Coeducation in Jamaica and the Caribbean cannot continue to ignore the research findings that conclude that both boys and girls perform better academically in single sex schools.

The political directorate – the ultimate decision makers – would not be elected to the Jamaican Parliament with a declared intention to keep black men and women marginal. On the contrary, they are elected with the express mandate to help the marginalized groups overcome marginality. In turn, marginal groups pin their greatest hope on education as the means of breaking away from the margins. Education policy making therefore becomes very sensitive politics. It is the failure of the politicians to assist the marginalized to realize their hopes that frequently brings about changes of government. Note must be taken of the frequency with which political mandates are repeatedly frustrated. The repetition of this cycle of hope and frustration has been sufficient to suggest that the processes at work are over and beyond the individual sincerity of politicians and bureaucrats.

Implications for External Assistance

External assistance is invariably couched in the rhetoric of redemption and liberation of the dispossessed. It would appear, however, that by and large, these interventions have strengthened the status quo, the position of the centrals. With respect to external agencies, this suggests either colossal ignorance of local conditions, or overwhelming ineptitude, or tacit and benign agreement to maintain the ruling minorities. Given that no intervention is neutral, foreign donors cannot absolve themselves from the outcome of their interventions.

Certainly UNESCO, the World Bank, USAID, and CIDA, which aided and assisted successive Jamaican governments since 1962 in expanding education, cannot stand aloof from the fact that their interventions have left black males in Jamaica more marginal in the Jamaican society than their grandfathers were. The full implications of this are still to be experienced. The recency of these interventions makes it still early to realize fully the entire extent of the social repercussions for family life, employment, religion, relations between the sexes, and the social structure.

Of equal importance is the fact that currently international aid agencies have invariably included women's issues as one of the conditionalities of development cooperation. While there is no gainsaying women's continued marginality in society, to address this issue without recognition that some men are as marginal or even more marginal than many women, is to embark upon lopsided policies in relation to gender.

Agencies have operated on the mistaken assumption that even though there is no equality of the sexes in industrialized society, the situation is even worse in the Third World. The goal of the Third World is to catch up with the industrialized world. Certainly with respect to the liberation of women, the Jamaican society is in advance of most industrialized countries. From the data produced in this study, boys are indeed the second sex in education from basic school to university. Current conditionalities and approaches advocated by multilateral and bilateral aid agencies are likely to be inappropriate in Jamaica.

It would appear also that development has been too narrowly conceived in terms of economic growth, without a broader vision of the social and cultural interrelationships. Some rethinking and redirection is necessary in development cooperation and in the conceptualization of gender issues.

Implications for the Women's Movement

Over the last thirty years there has been increasing awareness of women's issues and recognition of the feminist movement in the Jamaican society. While Jamaican women have long battled their marginalization in society, the feminist movement cannot claim to be indigenous, and in many instances liberated Jamaican women disclaim being feminists.

To feminists any formulation which suggests that men could be disadvantaged in any way, could be interpreted as being either invalid or as being a challenge to the women's movement itself. The danger of such a response would be to ignore important dimensions of the situation of men and women in the Jamaican society. Black men and women of all races occupy a similar social niche. In many ways they are marginalized with respect to mainstream society and the mechanisms used to keep them marginalized bear a striking resemblance. The similarity of their situation warrants cooperation and not conflict. For either to deny the marginality of the other is to fly in the face of reality.

In addition, several hardships faced by Jamaican women are a direct consequence of the precarious situation of the black man. Meaningful solutions must address the dilemmas of both men and women and not just one or the other. The issue is gender, not simply men's or women's position in society. This is particularly so when it comes to the socialization of both boys and girls. Increasingly it is the question of the redefinition and reconstruction of gender that must be addressed.

From one point of view, the marginalization process in Jamaica has created a strong women's lobby. The question is whether women will assault the marginalization process itself or defend the status quo and their place in it.

Another danger to be avoided is for black men to interpret their increasingly precarious position in society as the fault of women; that is, to believe that their increasing marginality in society is brought about by women, particularly black women. Even worse would be for black men to see the redress of the problems facing them in terms of the return of women to the private sphere of the home and to their historical and traditional roles as wives and mothers.

Likewise, women must resist the temptation to accept blame for the increasing marginalization of some men in society. Simplistic interpretations of the complex issues involved in the changing gender roles and relations should be avoided at all cost. Men and women need to take full account of the complexity of the phenomena outlined in this study, and from that starting point intentionally seek to construct a more just society.

CONCLUSION

One conclusion from this study is that the marginalization of black men in society is not a result of some unique features of black culture, biological endowment, or racism. Rather, it is a feature of the place structure of societies in which race and gender are among the criteria on which the society is organized, and in which Blacks are among the subordinate groups in those societies.

Further, the movement towards integration and away from segregation of ethnic groups seems to involve differential rates of incorporation of males and females of the subordinate groups into the mainstream of society. Again, young members of the subordinate groups appear to have greater chances of incorporation than older members. These differential rates of the incorporation of young members versus old, and males versus females, leave some young males of the subordinate group in an increasingly marginalized position.

Put plainly, the marginalization of black males is not a phenomenon that is peculiar to Blacks. Black males are among the first to experience this phenomenon on a massive scale because, in the New World, Blacks have been the first subordinate group to challenge successfully and gain concessions with respect to meaningful prospects for upward social mobility in society.

The experience of black males will be suffered increasingly by males of subordinate groups in patriarchal societies, whatever the other criteria by which the particular society is organized. In other words, the situation of black males will increasingly become the common experience of many men in modern society, however the particular modern society is organized. Specifically, the Jamaican case study should share common features with and be of relevance and interest to the following:

— The past and current experience of most black and lower-class men in Caribbean societies.
— The growing experience of Indian men, especially from rural areas, in Trinidad and Guyana.
— The past and current experience of black men in the United States.
— The unfolding experience of Hispanic, native American and poor white men in the United States.
— The past experience of non-communist Slavic men and non-Slavic men in the former Soviet Union.
— The likely experience of black and Indian men in South Africa and Southern Africa generally.

Turning to the Jamaican case study, the question could be asked with respect to directions to be taken in the future. From the perspective of place theory, the preconditions for the emergence of an authentic society which generates, in addition to its own internal source of power, an equitable distribution of wealth, status related to the value of a person's contribution to society, a belief system that legitimizes a just social order, and a culture that routinizes healthy relations between all members of the society, would be the following:

(a) the severance or neutralization by the ruling minority of all external power connections used by that minority to maintain itself without reference to or negotiation with the other social groups in the society;

(b) a decentralized democratic system of government which operates on the basis of the participation of all groups in the decision-making process and regards negotiations as the basis of settling differences and disputes;

(c) the redefinition of gender and gender roles in society and the corresponding modification of the socialization by men and women of all social and ethnic groups in the society; and

(d) a restructuring of the institutional arrangements so as to ensure equity and fairness in the access to opportunity by men and women of all ethnic groups from all social segments and all geographic areas.

These are elements, not necessarily in the order presented, which appear to be crucial in any framework for restructuring the social order and gender in the Jamaican society.

Bibliography

Aldrich, Richard. 1982. *Introduction to the History of Education*. London: Hodder and Stoughton.

Allen, Grant. 1904. *In All Shades*. London: Chatto and Windus.

Amos, Valerie, and Pratibha Parmar. 1984. "Challenging Imperial Feminism". *Feminist Review* 17: 3-20.

Barrett, Michelle, and Mary McIntosh. 1985. "Ethnocentrism and Socialist-Feminist Theory". *Feminist Review* 20 (Summer): 23-48.

Black, Clinton V. 1958. *History of Jamaica*. London: Collins.

"Black Men: Mean Streets". 1990. CNN Documentary: (3-6 September).

Bolland, Nigel O. 1977. *Formation of a Colonial Society: Belize, from Conquest to Crown Colony*. Baltimore: Johns Hopkins University Press.

Brathwaite, Edward. 1971. *The Development of Creole Society in Jamaica: 1770-1820*. Oxford: Clarendon Press.

Braverman Harry. 1979. *Labor and Monoply Capital: The Degradation of Work in the Twentieth Century*. New York: Monthly Review Press.

Bryans, H. 1974. "Virtuous Women at Half-Price: The Feminization of Teachers in Ontario in the late Nineteenth Century". Master in Education Thesis. University of Toronto.

Campbell, Carl. 1963. "The Development of Primary Education in Jamaica 1834-1865". Master's Thesis, London University/University of the West Indies.

_______ . 1967. "Towards an Imperial Policy for the Education of Negroes in the West Indies After Emancipation". *Jamaica Histroical Review* 7: 68-102.

_______ . 1970. "Social and Economic Obstacles to the Development of Popular Education in Post-Emancipation Jamaica, 1834-1865". *Journal of Caribbean History* 1 (November): 57-88.

Census of Jamaica. 1871 to 1943.

Cundall, Frank. 1914. *The Mico College: Jamaica*. Kingston.

Curtin, Phillip D. 1955. *Two Jamaicas: The Role of Ideas in a Tropical Colony 1830-1865*. Cambridge: Harvard University Press.

Dev, Shirley. 1985. *The Sexual Division of Work*. Brighton: Harvester Press.

D'Oyley, Vincent. 1979. "Plans and Progress in Nineteenth Century Jamaican Teacher Education". In *Development and Disillusion in Third World Education*, edited by Vincent D'Oyley and Reginald Murray. Toronto: The Ontario Institute for Studies in Education.

Eisner, Gisela. 1961. *Jamaica, 1830-1930: A Study in Economic Growth*. Connecticut: Greenwood Press.

Foster, Phillip. 1982. "The Education Policies of Post-Colonial States". In *Education and Development*, edited by Lascelles Anderson and Douglas M. Windham. London: D.C. Heath and Company.

Froude, James Anthony. 1888. *The English in the West Indies*. London: Charles Scribner & Sons.

Gordon, Derek. 1987. *Class, Status and Social Mobility in Jamaica*. Kingston: Institute of Social and Economic Research, UWI.

_______ . 1989. "Class, Race and Social Mobility in Jamaica". In *Garvey: His Work and Impact*, edited by R. Lewis and P. Bryan. Kingston: ISER and Extra Mural Dept.

_______ . 1991. "Access to High School Education in Post-War Jamaica". In *Education and Society in the Commonwealth Caribbean*, edited by Errol Miller. Mona, Jamaica: Institute of Social and Economic Research, UWI.

Gordon, Shirley. 1963. *A Century of West Indian Education*. London: Longman.

_______ . 1968. *Reports and Repercussions in West Indian Education 1835-1935*. London: Ginn and Company Ltd.

Goulbourne, Harry. 1988. *Teachers, Education and Politics in Jamaica 1892-1972*. London: Macmillan.

Greene, Edward J. 1993. "Race, Class and Gender in the Future of the Caribbean: An Overview". In *Race, Class and Gender in the Future of the Caribbean*, edited by J. Edward Greene, 1-14. Mona, Jamaica: Institute of Social and Economic Research, UWI.

Hamilton, Marlene A. 1985. "Performance Levels in Science and Other Subjects for Jamaican Adolescents Attending Single Sex and Co-educational High Schools". *Science Education* 69, no.4: 535-47.

Hark, Walter, and Adolphus Westphal. 1904. *Breaking of the Dawn, Moravian Work in Jamaica*. London: William Strain and Sons.

Hartman, Heidi I. 1979. "Capitalism, Patriarchy and Job Segregation by Sex". In *Capitalist Patriarchy*, edited by Zillah R. Eistenstein. New York: Monthly Review Press.

_______ . 1981. "The Unhappy Marriage of Marxism and Feminism: Towards a More Progressive Union". In *Women and Liberation*, edited by Lydia Sargent. London: Pluto Press.

Herskovits, Melville. 1941. *The Myth of the Negro Past*. New York: Harpers.

Heuman, Gad J. 1981. *Between Black and White: Race, Politics and the Free Coloureds in Jamaica 1792-1865*. Connecticut: Greenwood Press.

International Labor Organization. 1989. *Women in the World of Work*.

Jacobs, H.P. 1973. *Sixty Years of Change, 1806-1866*. Kingston: Institute of Jamaica.

King, Ruby H. 1972. "History of the Jamaica Schools Commission: Its Role in Education in Jamaica, 1879 to 1911". Master's (Education) thesis, UWI (Mona).

Kuper, Adam. 1976. *Changing Jamaica*. Kingston: Kingston Publishers.

La Guerre, J. G. 1993. "A Review of Race and Class in the Caribbean". In *Race, Class and Gender in the Future of the Caribbean*, edited by J. Edward Greene. Mona, Jamaica: Institute of Social and Economic Research, UWI.

Levy, Claude. 1980. *Emancipation, Sugar and Federalism: Barbados and the West Indies 1833-1876*. Gainesville: University of Florida Press.

Livingstone, W.P. 1900. *Black Jamaica*. London.

Louis, Errol T. 1985. "Black Male Unemployment". *Essence* (March): 99 -103, 138-40.

Lowenthal, David. 1972. *West Indian Societies*. London: Oxford University Press.

Manley, Douglas. 1963. "Mental Ability in Jamaica". *Social and Economic Studies* 12, no.1: 51-71.

Martin, D. 1976. *Jamaica National Literacy Programme: Project Findings and Recommendations*. Paris: UNESCO.

Massiah, Joycelyn. 1987. "The Cultural Reality of Caribbean Women's Working Lives". Paper prepared for the First Interdisciplinary Seminar, Women and Development Studies, Mona, 8-19 June 1987.

Miller, Errol. 1976. "Education and Society in Jamaica". In *Sociology of Education: A Caribbean Reader*, edited by Peter M. Figueroa and Ganga Persaud. Oxford: Oxford University Press.

_______ . 1990. *Jamaican Society and High Schooling*. Mona, Jamaica: Institute of Social and Economic Research, UWI.

_______ . 1991. *Men at Risk*. Kingston: Jamaica Publishing House.

_______ . 1992. *Education for All: Caribbean Perspectives and Imperatives*. Washington, D.C.: Inter-American Development Bank. Distributed by Johns Hopkins University Press.

Mills, Charles. W. 1993. "A Comment on Race, Class and Gender – The Unholy Trinity". In *Race, Class and Gender in the Future of the Caribbean*, edited by J. Edward Greene. Mona, Jamaica: Institute of Social and Economic Research, UWI.

Morrissey, Michael P. 1984. "A Rural-Urban Stratification of Jamaica for Sampling Procedures". *Social and Economics Studies* 33, no.4: 101-23.

Munroe, Sylvester. 1987. "Brothers". *Newsweek* (23 March): 55.

Newman, A. J. 1974. "Mico Training College". *Torch* 1, no. 2 (October 1974): 12-14.

Newton, Velma. 1984. *The Silver Men: West Indian Labour Migration to Panama 1850-1914*. Mona, Jamaica: Institute of Social and Economic Research, UWI.

Owens, Joseph. 1976. *Dread: the Rastafarians of Jamaica*. Kingston: Sangsters.

Patterson, Orlando. 1967. *Sociology of Slavery*. London: MacGibbon and Kee Ltd.

Phillipo, J.M. 1843. *Jamaica: Its Past and Present State*. London: John Snow.

Phillippo, J.C. 1883, *Jamaica: Its Government and People*. Kingston.

Reddock, Rhoda. 1993. "The Primacy of Gender in Race and Class". In *Race, Class and Gender and the Future of the Caribbean*, edited by J. Edward Greene. Mona, Jamaica: Institute of Social and Economic Research, UWI.

Savage, John 1877. *A Brief Sketch of Education in Jamaica*. House of Commons Parliamentary Papers. Vol. LIX.

Sharbodie, Derrick. 1992. "Being a Real Man – Like Mom". *Trinidad Express*.

Smith M.G. 1965. *The Plural Society in the British West Indies*. Berkeley and Los Angeles: University of California Press.

_______ . 1984. *Culture, Race and Class in the Commonwealth Caribbean*. Kingston: Department of Extra Mural Studies, University of the West Indies.

Smith, Raymond T. 1961. "Review of Social and Cultural Pluralism in the Caribbean". *American Anthropologist* 63: 155-57.

_______ . 1967. "Social Stratification, Cultural Pluralism and Integration in West Indian Societies". In *Caribbean Integration: Papers on Social, Political and Economic Integration*, 226-358. Rio Piedras, Puerto Rico: Institute of Caribbean Studies.

Staples, Robert. 1987. "Black Male Genocide: A Final Solution to the Race Problem in America". *The Black Scholar* 18, no. 3 (May/June): 2-11.

Tyack, David B., and Myra H. Strober. 1981. "Jobs and Gender: A History of Education Employment by Sex". In *Educational Policy and Management: Sex Differential*, edited by Patricia Schmuck, W. Charles and Richard Carlson. New York: Academic Press Inc.

Tyack, David B., and Elizabeth Hansot. 1982. *Managers of Virtue: Public School Leadership in America, 1820-1980*. New York: Basic Books.

Vincent, Francis X. 1978. "Some Factors Associated with Achievement in Literacy Among Adults in Jamaica". Master's thesis, University of the West Indies.

Walby, Sylvia. 1990. *Theorizing Patriarchy*. Oxford: Basil Blackwell Ltd.

White, Millicent. 1977. *A Short History of Education in Jamaica*. London: Hodder and Stoughton.

Wint, Carl. 1989. "Where Have All the Men Gone?" *Newsletter of the Population Policy Coordinating Committee* 1, no. 2: 1-2.

Official Documents and Papers

Annual and General Departmental Reports Department of Education, Jamaica. 1880 - 1940.

Blue Books of Jamaica, 1867-1940.

Draft Five-Year Plan: 1978-1983.

The Education Sector Survey: 1971.

The Education Thrust of the Seventies: 1973.

Elementary and Secondary Education Law. 1892.

The Five-Year Independence Plan: 1963-1968.

Handbook of Jamaica. 1881.

Jamaica. Civil Service Examinations 1894. House of Commons Parliamentary Papers Col 137/561 XC14385.

Joint Board of Teacher Education. 1982. *Regulations.* Kingston, Mona: University of the West Indies.

Kandel, I. L. 1943. *Report of the Committee Appointed to Enquire into the System of Secondary Education in Jamaica.*

Latrobe, C. J. 1837. *Report from C.J. Latrobe to the Right Hon. Lord Glenelg on Negro Education in Jamaica.*

Report of the Educational Planning Mission: Jamaica, September-November 1964. Paris: UNESCO, 1965.

The Lumb Commission Report 1898. Jamaica Commission to Enquire into the System of Education (Chief Justice Charles F. Lumb, Chairman).

The National Development Plan for Education 1990-1995.

The National Plan: 1957-67.

The New Deal for Education. 1966. Kingston: Government Printing Office.

Proceedings of the Jamaica Legislative Council 1880-1900.

Report on Jamaica. 1956. Kingston: Government Printing Office.

Report on the Condition of the Juvenile Population in Jamaica, 1879. In *Reports and Repercussions in West Indian Education 1835-1935*, Shirley Gordon. London: Ginn and Company Ltd. 1968.

Reports and Statistics of the Congregations of the United Brethrens of Moravians at Fairfield. 1895.

The Reverend John Sterling's Report. 1835. Extracts. In *Reports and Repercussions in West Indian Education 1835-1935*, Shirley Gordon. London: Ginn and Company Ltd. 1968.

The 10-Year Plan of Development for Jamaica: 1947-1957.

Trust Deed of the Calabar College, 1904. Held by the Jamaica Baptist Union, Kingston , Jamaica.

Report of the West Indies Royal Commission: 1884. (William Crossman, Chairman).